Esther
Whiteley's 25.6.90

THE SACRED

THE SACRED IN LIFE AND ART

BY

PHILIP SHERRARD

GOLGONOOZA PRESS

Published by Golgonooza Press
3 Cambridge Drive, Ipswich IP2 9EP, U.K.

British Library Cataloguing in Publication Data
Sherrard, Philip
The sacred in life and art.
1. Religion
I. Title
200

ISBN 0 903880 41 5 *cloth*
ISBN 0 903880 42 3 *paper*

Typeset by Goodfellow & Egan, Cambridge
Printed by St Edmundsbury Press

To

Rory & Julie

with love

CONTENTS

PREFACE

✠

The chapters that form the text of this book are related one to the other more by congeneracy and convergence of theme than by continuity of argument. That they are all concerned in one way or another with the sacred—either with trying to understand its nature, or with exploring the conditions under which it may be avowed in our life and in our art; or with elucidating the consequences of our failure so to avow it. The concept of a completely profane world—of a cosmos wholly desacralized—is a fairly recent invention of the human mind, while the endeavour to implement it in practical terms by erecting it into the standard according to which we determine the major forms of our social, economic, political and personal life, is still more recent—in fact only now are we becoming aware of the enormity of the self-destruction that it involves. The invention of the concept itself, as well as the endeavour to implement it, presuppose of course that we first blind our intellectual sight with a sacrilegious and hence totally fraudulent notion of the physical universe—with, in other words, the cataract of modern science. That is why the attempt to recover the integrity of our thought and vision must begin with the removal of this opaque secretion—something to which the final chapter is particularly dedicated. But this attempt can lead to a reversal of the present suicidal flow of things only if it is a consequence of and is accompanied by the re-awakening in ourselves of a consciousness of the meaning and presence of the sacred, in all its manifestations. The purpose of this book is to make some slight contribution to such a re-awakening.

Philip Sherrard
Katounia, Limni, Evia.
December 1989.

1

PRESUPPOSITIONS OF THE SACRED

✠

The word 'sacred' is one of a whole group of cognate words—words like sacrament, sacrilege, sacrosanct, consecrate, sacrifice—the original meaning of this last, sacrifice, being precisely to 'make sacred' (*sacra facere*). Its root, then, is Latin, not Greek: 'sacer', still present in our sacerdotal, of or pertaining to a priest; and it denotes something set apart, devoted to a deity, a holy offering. In early Christian language it was applied in its synonymous form, *sacramentum,* to any action or object which as mirror or vehicle or form of the Divine was regarded as revealing the Divine. We are at once in the midst of things. The sacred is something in which the Divine is present or which is charged with divine energies. That the very idea of the sacred presupposes to start with the presence of the Divine or the existence of God. Without the Divine—without God—there can be no holiness, nothing sacred. We cannot talk about the sacred without presupposing God, just as we cannot talk about sunlight without presupposing the sun, however many mirrors it may be reflected in.

Moreover, God is not only the principle—the original cause—of all making sacred. He alone is sacred. At one of the most solemn moments in the divine liturgy of the Orthodox Church the priest raises the consecrated bread before the congregation and cries: 'Holy things to those who are holy'; whereupon the congregation responds: 'Only One is holy, only One is Lord, Christ in the glory of God the Father'. The presence of God is, that is to say, the initial and ultimately unique presupposition of the sacred, for the simple reason that without that presence there is no sacredness anywhere. This means that if, for instance, earth, nature, life, art, or anything else is sacred, this is because it is the expression or revelation of something infinitely more than itself, something which it but discloses or manifests. It is not because it is sacred in its own right, apart from this Other that it enshrines, still less because we make it sacred. The first symptom of the profane mind—of the idolatrous mind—is its habit of separating its ideas of things from the idea of God; because as soon as you do begin to separate these ideas from the idea of God you have set out on the path that leads to the desacralization, the desecration and ultimately to the destruction of the things themselves.

If, then, something in the physical or psychological realm—the realm in which we experience the greater part of what we do experience—is sacred, this is because God, the wholly Other, has irrupted into or ingressed upon it. The sacred, in so far as we experience it, presupposes—and this is its second presupposition—the ingression of that which is wholly Other upon the physical or psychological realm. This posits a theme crucial to the understanding of the sacred: the theme of the transcendent.

This theme may be introduced by way of a comment. In much contemporary literature that speaks of a new approach to things—that speaks of mankind having reached a turning-point or being about to enter a new age, the age of Aquarius or the solar age—one frequently comes across the word whole, or holistic: we are asked to see things as a whole, in all the complexity of their multi-interrelationships, and not as isolated, fragmented, non-participative phenomena or substances, which is the way we have been conditioned to see them over the last few centuries.

This is excellent, so far as it goes. But it doesn't go as far as the point that would make it really meaningful. Because the interrelationships that are spoken of and the wholeness which they are said to constitute appear to be confined to the psychological and physical realms alone. That which lies beyond this realm—the transcendent—appears to be tacitly left out of account, almost as if it were irrelevant to the *real* world with which modern science, including the so-called new physics and parapsychology, is concerned.

Yet to talk about wholeness, or the holistic approach to things, without including within one's perspective that which lies beyond the psychological and physical realm, is to put the cart before the horse. For just as there can be nothing sacred without God, because ultimately God alone is sacred, so there can be no wholeness without God, because ultimately God alone is whole. It is God that is the principle and source of wholeness, and without participation in God there can be no escaping fragmentation, disintegration, self-alienation, however much we may struggle against them. In Greek the words which correspond to the English words save, salvation, Saviour, contain the sense both of soundness and of wholeness. To be saved is to attain a state in which one is sound and whole, entire; and the Saviour is He who bestows these qualities—who integrates, makes whole, keeps alive and well—because they are qualities that belong to Him and to no-one and nothing else. That is why when we lose contact with God, or when we ignore the transcendent, we not only cut ourselves off from the source of sacredness but also, and as a consequence, fall into a state of sickness and self-division.

Indeed, it is this losing contact with God, the source of holiness and wholeness, that is the crux of the fall of man; and our modern age exemplifies it as perhaps no other age ever has, because it is the product of a state of mind which has lost the sense not only of this fall but also and correspondingly of practically every aspect of the sacred. A symptom, if not the cause, of this disastrous state of mind may be discerned already in the famous doctrine of the 'double truth' proposed in the Middle Ages by the scholastic philosophers. According to this doctrine there is a double order in things, a double order of knowledge, or two levels on which things are viewable. There is a supranatural order, and there is a natural order (nature now being understood as a purely physical reality). The supranatural order is the state in which grace is paramount, and it corresponds to the sphere of theology. But where nature is concerned, no considerations of grace or divine intervention are necessary, because nature follows its own inherent laws which have nothing to do with grace or divine intervention. This means that nature—the natural as such—is now accorded a status of its own, to all intents and purposes independent of God. Of course, by the scholastic philosophers God is still regarded as the author of nature, but essentially nature works according to its own laws, and it is quite sufficient to take account only of these laws in order to discover how nature does work.

Moreover, it is now assumed that these laws can be investigated and defined by the human reason quite apart from whether or not this reason is itself illumined by divine grace or inspiration. In other words, in order to discover the laws of nature—to gain a knowledge of nature—neither divine grace nor divine illumination is necessary. Such a view of things at once gives a charter to the unregenerate and profane human mind to study and investigate nature as though there was nothing divine in it or about it at all, and even more disastrously it gives assurance to such a mind that the knowledge it obtains as the result of its observation and investigation is a valid and authentic sort of knowledge. This charter and this assurance are the prerequisites and mainsprings of the modern scientific mentality, which actually demands that we regard the physical world, man and practically everything else as impersonal objects, deprived of all divine qualities and possessing nothing sacred about them at all. A mentality such as this builds a world in its own image: our own mechanized, industrialized, dehumanized and desacralized world, in which man's separation from God not only alienates him from himself but also separates the visible universe from man and makes both of them wanderers, lost travellers cast out into the deserts of time and space.

At this point it may be protested that I am exposing myself to something like a contradiction. I have said that the initial presupposition of the sacred is the reality of God and of a divine realm lying beyond the psychological and physical realm, while the second presupposition is the irruption of this transcendent divine reality—the wholly Other—into the psychological and physical realm. But if this is the case, what is wrong, it may be asked, with the scholastic distinction between two orders of things—the supranatural and natural orders—which I claim has had such disastrous consequences for both man and nature and has finally led to the virtual obliteration of our sense of the sacred altogether? Am I not affirming precisely the same kind of distinction when I speak of a divine realm that *transcends* the psychological and physical realm, even though it may irrupt into the latter? And in that case, what is wrong in studying and investigating the natural order, and man along with it, as though they were objects obedient to their own laws which are quite other than the laws—if there are any—which operate in the transcendent order? What is wrong in separating the idea of nature from the idea of God? Why can't there be theology on the one hand, and science on the other?

This introduces us to the third presupposition of the sacred: the presupposition not of God's transcendence to nature, but of the mutual immanence—the mutual indwellingness—of God and nature, the interpenetration of the uncreated and the created. 'Theology' is a word which has become somewhat debased coinage in our age. For us it tends to mean something abstract, something that goes on in universities or among congeries of bishops: we call it 'God-talk' or something equally disparaging. Yet actually it denotes far more than learning and discourse about God and religious doctrine acquired through academic study. 'In the beginning was the Word.' So opens the authorized English version of St John's Gospel. But what is translated into English here as Word is the Greek word *logos*, and *logos* in Greek means far more than Word does in English. *Logos* betokens the underlying reality of things, that which they are, or that which is, before their appearance, or that of which their appearance is the manifestation. And St John's Gospel goes on, in the same sentence, 'and the *logos* was God'—*kai Theos in o logos*. 'Theology'—from these two words, God and Logos—is to do therefore with the underlying divine reality of things and personal participation in it. If I speak of nature as theological I mean precisely this: that its underlying reality is divine and that it participates in this divinity. If I speak of man's existence as theological I mean the same thing. In this sense 'theological' means more even than 'theophanic', which is the showing forth of God, the showing forth of the divine; it means the actual symbiosis—living together—of the uncreated and the created, the Divine and the human, God and nature.

We are here in a sphere of understanding which lies far beyond that to which we are accustomed, in so far as we think about these things at all. When people talk about God—and this is especially true perhaps in the Christian world—they often talk about Him as if He were a kind of object. And if they go on to talk about the relationship between God and the world, they often talk about it as being above all a relationship of cause and effect: God is a world cause, a final cause or principle of being and existence; and the world and its laws are what He has produced. We are in the sphere of understanding which makes it possible for us to accept the scholastic distinction between the two orders or levels of existence, the one supranatural and the other natural. Admittedly, we can still speak of some analogy between these two orders, between God and creation. We can still speak in Platonic terms of creation, like time, as a 'moving image of eternity' or in Hermetic terms of what is below being like what is above. We can still say that signs and indications of God—vestiges or signatures of God—may be discerned in visible phenomena, or that the visible world is a kind of divine cryptogram that we have to decipher. But in this view of things it is difficult for us to go beyond that and to escape from what one might call a dualistic mentality, for which the otherness of God is projected in the otherness of the physical or material nature of the visible world, so that there is always a distance between them, a hiatus which culminates in an absence—in a *deus absconditus*—and makes it impossible to conceive of a nuptial union between them.

For this type of mentality, as well as for the Gnostic type of mentality, the miracle of this union will always remain inconceivable or illusory, or at best the outward showing of something whose true reality must be sought on another level. The miracle is that the divine Otherness becomes for me more interior than my own soul. Experienced in this way, God is never an object. He can be known only through Himself becoming the absolute subject of my own being—through an epiphany or incarnation which in its own right displaces my ego or selfhood and puts in its place this absolute subject who is God. This means that, paradoxical as it may sound, it is ultimately myself, in so far as God has become the absolute subject of my being, that reveals God to me, free from all spurious objectivity. At the same time—and this is the other aspect of the same paradox—the divine subject is always the active subject of all knowledge of God. This is why to revere God's gifts in other people is the same thing as to revere God Himself.

And so it is with everything in creation. Not only man but every created thing bears a hidden divine *logos* or essence so at one with its concrete appearance that there is an intimate interpenetration, a secret coincidence between them. By mutual assimilation Creator and created, the visible form and the divine idea informing it, grow together to the point at which each becomes the other's mine: the two become one. It is as in the sacrament of marriage in which the beloved otherness of the two partners itself constitutes the matter or ground of the sacrament: *finis amoris ut duo unam fiant*. It is not a case of the complete absorption of the one in the other, or of subservience on the one side and detachment on the other. Moreover, the created depends on the uncreated, while the reverse is not the case. But each finds its own identity in the other, and each at the same time keeps its own identity in the other. It is a union which, although it overcomes division, does not involve confusion.

In creating what is created, it is Himself that God creates, in another form. In creation, He becomes His own symbol: the image is also epiphany. To symbolic realism corresponds epiphanic realism. The created image, that is to say, far from being merely the image that suggests or points to an intelligible reality, actually contains and expresses this reality. It does not merely signify; it *is* what it signifies. A tree, for instance, is an intelligible reality that thinks itself in the form of a tree. Creation is a revelation not simply of a truth about God; it is the revelation of God Himself: 'The heavens declare the glory of God', 'heaven and earth are full of Thy glory'. The created world is God's sacrifice, His transmutation of Himself in His creatures: it is the means whereby He is what He is. Were there no creation, then God would be other than He is; and if creation were not sacramental, then God would not be its creator and there would be nothing sacramental or sacred anywhere. If God is not present in a grain of sand He is not present in heaven either.

Yet in all this there is no question of pantheism—pantheism always tends to involve idolatry and to demean both God, man and nature as a whole. What there is, on the other hand, is a panentheism—an immanence which we may experience and express as God being present in creation but which is really that of creation being present in God, as the unborn child is present in the mother. Once again, it is not a matter of the reflection of God in creation or in the physical universe, in the sense that implies that there is a relationship of parallelism or mutual analogies between them, or even resemblances and correspondences, as many modern commentators on these matters tend to express it, generally on the authority of the Hermetic formula, 'As above, so below', to which I have already referred. What is in question is a relationship one might describe as a dialectic of the unity of opposites—a unity in the duality of Spirit and matter that unites them in a manner that goes beyond all monism just as radically as it goes beyond the dualist two principles of ultimate explanation, or the notion that objects exist only in so far as they are perceived by the cognitive subject.

If, then, divine transcendence is one presupposition of the sacred, so equally is immanence in God. There is no dichotomy between God and creation, no dualism, no double order of things which makes it legitimate to study the world of phenomena as though it were to all intents and purposes independent of God. To study the world of phenomena in this way is only possible when in our minds we have already denaturalized nature. Nature—the psycho-physical realm—can be understood only when we recognize the reciprocal immanence of God and man, the uncreated and the created universe. But if there is no dichotomy, no dualism, there is duality. Dualism connotes the opposition, the externality of two units. It connotes irreducible pluralism with two terms. Duality on the other hand indicates the mutual completion of two units. It means two in one, two in so far as they go to make one. It is a partnership not merely for outward action but also and above all for reciprocal reaction, interaction: a link that binds two units together in their very being, and turns them towards each other. Each depends on the presence of the other either in order to be or at least in order to be fully. And this is so even when there is, as there is between God and man, God and creation, subordination and inequality, even when the reciprocity is not equal on both sides. For if the lower receives its existence and keeps its value from the higher, the higher receives its full meaning, is shaped into a Self and is personalized by the lower. The reciprocity holds good. The world of phenomena is also the theophanic world in which God shows Himself forth. It is not illusion: it is the other self of the Absolute and so an aspect of Reality itself. Short of realizing this one will always remain outside the realm of the sacred. So long as one thinks that there is on the one hand a subject, an 'I' isolated in its egoness and set over against the world of phenomena, and on the other hand an object, God, a divine Being isolated and abstracted in its unknowability, there cannot be any access to the sacred, whether in life or art.

Transcendence and immanence are thus correlative, not contradictory terms. Without transcendence there is no immanence, but equally without immanence there is no transcendence. And they do not make a double reality, or multiply reality into two. They may be distinct in their formal aspects or functions. The transcendent, as subject, may never be enclosed by the immanent. The immanent—the lower—may be immanent in the transcendent—the higher—where its very being is concerned, while this is not the case for the higher, just as the immanence of the child in the mother is for the child a matter of life or death while this is not the case for the mother. But in spite of these differences, each of the elements of the partnership—God and man, the Divine and nature—is, or represents, not simply the same reality, but that reality in its fullness. Each is, or represents, both the whole and the same whole. And it is their vital conjunction, their dynamic interpenetration, which gives birth to the sacred and makes the whole visible universe theological, the matter of a sacrament, a single icon of God, a holocaust of divine love and beauty.

If this then is the reality of things, how is it that we so abysmally fail to perceive it as such and to experience it as such? How is it that we have built around ourselves a world that witnesses to the desecration of this reality at every point and at every moment—a desecration that we perpetrate without even realizing that we are desecrating anything or that there is anything to desecrate? The temple-robbers of old at least were aware that they were robbing temples; we have lost even the sense that there is a temple to rob, a temple to profane, and this gives us an impunity to commit our crimes, our day's work of slaughter and pillage, methodically, without passion, as one might prune or operate, and with no sense of guilt. We have stripped inner and outer landscape bare of all those emblems of sanctity, those recollections of sanctity, which once nourished the soul—the shrines of saints, the retreats of hermits and holy men, their sanctuaries of worship and prayer, the festivals of song and dance in which they were celebrated. And even if sometimes we borrow their ideas to spice a discourse, to give an air of sophistication to our art or scholarship, it is much in the manner of Heliogabulus who ate the brains of ostriches, and not at all with the sense that it is their lives that we should be emulating. Indeed, so far from emulating their lives we continue to cut the cloth of our mind and body not in order to be worthy of the kingdom of heaven but in order to fit more comfortably into our comfortless and uprooted world.

And if we ask—and to our credit we are beginning to ask it more and more—in the name of what have we reduced ourselves to such caricatures, to such parodies of our true stature, inflicting the same distortion on to everything about us, we will find in the end that it is in the name of that mentality, with its pitiful complement of basic concepts, which is still committed to perpetuating this state of affairs; which still persuades us that we have the right, if not the duty, to invade and ransack the physical world at any and every point—to split atoms, dissect living animals, defile the sky, experiment with gene and foetus, and in laboratories, power-stations and factories to prepare those fruits—and by their fruits you shall know them—whose brutal inhumanity testifies only too well to the infernal source from which they derive. We will find that we have despoiled our inheritance in the name of a science that exists and can exist only through the appalling negation of all wisdom and true philosophy, the elimination of the person as of every other sacred reality, and a criminal indifference as to whether or not God is active in human and other life and human and other life are active in God. One might have thought that if we cannot have pity on man and the birds and the trees and the flowers, at least we might echo the recruiting cry of the crusaders: Man, have pity upon God. But there we are more silent even than the stones.

Meanwhile we are all actors out of work, with no part to play. We have even totally forgotten that we have a part to play, let alone how to play it—our part in a sacred drama which alone can confer meaning and beauty on our lives—and that unless we do play this part we disrupt the harmony not only of our own lives but also the life of everything about us.

For that interplay of the uncreated and the created, the invisible and the visible, the transcendent and the immanent, which constitutes the sacred, presupposes the participation of man just as much as it presupposes the activity of God. This is a further presupposition of the sacred. Man's role is crucial in the actualization of the sacred not so much because he is a vital link in the chain of Being that extends from higher to lower down the whole scale of creation, as because he is a microtheos—a lesser god—in a microcosm. This is to say that man is not simply one created being, however exalted, among other created beings. He is not simply the microcosm in whom all that exists in the physical world is subsumed and summed up, in such a way that one can affirm that the physical world is simply the human soul writ large. He is also himself the macrocosm, the measure of all things, and the physical world is his creation just as God is his principle. This means that we perceive the physical world correctly ('not with but thro' the eye') when we know it as the living, richly varied but scattered 'portions of Man's immortal body'. In other words, just as we can speak, not of pantheism, but of panentheism—of all things indwelling in God—so we can speak, not of pananthropism, but of panenanthropism—of all things existing in man. It is when we forget this, and think of God as our judge and nature as our mother, that we go astray.

This status of man in relation to the physical world makes his participation in the process of 'making sacred'—his participation in the sacrificial rite—as much a presupposition of its fulfilment as the activity of God. For although the physical world is so impregnated by divine energies that everything bears within it its own creative *logos* or essence, its hidden seed of divinity, this seed of divinity cannot come to fruition—cannot be brought from a state of potentiality to a state of actualization and revelation—without human cooperation. It is not that things—what we call material realities—are objects in the sense presupposed by modern science; but they remain in bondage, atrophied, stagnant, frustrated, unless they are animated by human sympathy and love. They attain their meaning, come to fruition and are fulfilled in human perception. It is through man as the knowing subject that they are felt, imagined and sanctified. It is in and through us that the physical world is hallowed and that its intrinsic sacramental quality is revealed. It is we who are the priests of the temple of this world. For if this world is a mode of discourse between man and God, or the revelation of God to man, giving the measure of the transcendent Unity in the variety of all things, then at the same time man is the organ through which—or through whom—God unveils to this world its own mysteries.

Yet we can only ourselves fulfil our priest-like task on condition that our own inner world is animated by God. That perception through which we can hallow things is not ours, or at least it is ours only in so far as we can go out of ourselves, not towards the physical world, but towards God. It is only when we can contemplate in ourselves the Wisdom of God, the beauty of the poetic essences of the universe, and in their light recognize their counterparts or equivalents hidden beneath the outward appearance of things, that we can reveal to these things their eternal being and bring this being to fruition.

For like responds only to like; so that unless our own perception of things is itself charged with the knowledge and love that have their source in God, the latent seeds of divinity in what we perceive will not find in us anything to respond to, and so will remain latent, in bondage, stagnant and frustrated, and we will have failed in our priestly role and will have profaned, not hallowed, the temple in which this making sacred—this holy sacrifice—is our responsibility. It is on us that creation depends. It is in our life that creation lives. This is what St Paul has in mind when he speaks of all creation groaning and travailing in pain, living in the hope of deliverance from the bondage of corruption and waiting expectantly for the revelation of the sons of God—waiting for man to transform it into a cosmic temple of adoration and praise.

It should now be clear why we so fail to realize and to experience the reality of things as they are, if only they were allowed to be what they are: it is because we fail to recognize and acknowledge, at least in effective existential terms, the bond that unites God and man, God and creation, and because for all our claims to the contrary we do not in fact act as though everything is, or can be, sacred. We divorce our ideas of things—our ideas of nature, life, art, knowledge whether scientific or other—from the idea of God. We do not contemplate in ourselves the forms of divine Wisdom, those spiritual forms which in essence are visible only to the eyes of the heart and in whose light alone we can perceive the holiness of things. For how we perceive things, or reveal them to ourselves, depends ultimately on the vision we have of our own inner being; and if that vision does not embrace the spiritual qualities—of beauty—of love, that fill our being when we attune ourselves to God, we cannot perceive these qualities in the forms of the things about us; we cannot perceive their intrinsic sacredness. The link between transcendence and immanence is broken. The intimate interpenetration, the secret coincidence of uncreated and created, divine archetype and visible image, is frustrated, and the marriage between them remains in a state of suspension.

Indeed, it may often be, and in our world certainly is, far worse than this. For the more we fail to attune ourselves to God, the more we begin to live according to the illusion that our own self is sufficient to itself in order to be itself. The more we fail to assimilate the forms of eternal Wisdom, the more we confine ourselves to the sphere of the psychological and the aesthetic and become, knowingly or in a state of delusion, victims of our limited intelligence, our hallucinatory imagination, our unstable emotions, our own purely individual and subjective reactions to what we perceive or come into contact with. The deep-seated amoralism of the human being, his internal chaos, is now unleashed by the irresistible and seductive power of the aesthetic impulses of the soul; and the images that they project into the imagination, far from having anything sacred about them, represent more and more an ontological perversion, a lack of coincidence between divine archetype and visible form, a dissolution of the bond uniting the divine and the human, the uncreated and the created, and an eclipse of inner content.

These images are no longer symbols, for a symbol unites the visible and the invisible, the terrestrial and the celestial, while these images but testify to the sundering in human consciousness of these two aspects of reality, to their throwing apart (and one should remember that in Greek the word symbol and the word devil have the same root, but that the one denotes a bringing together while the other denotes a throwing apart). And when such images inform and animate man's perception of and relationship with the physical world, or inform and animate his art, they produce not a revelation of the intrinsic sacredness of things, but a dislocation, a distortion that vilifies the very idea that life and art should be a bringing to birth of the beautiful and the holy.

Art is in fact a sphere in which discrimination between the sacred and the profane, the sanctifying and the degrading, is particularly difficult and where confusion is all too likely to occur. Assuredly, the presuppositions of the sacred of which I have already spoken apply also where a sacred quality in a work of art is concerned. But when talking about the first of these presuppositions—namely, that all sacredness has its source in God—I said that man himself cannot make something sacred: he can participate in the making sacred, but he cannot be the active agent. The active agent must always be God, so much so that in one sense man—the 'I' or 'ego'—does nothing.

Yet by virtue of the fact that man is created in the image of God, he is also a creator, a maker, an artist. Indeed, this is his distinguishing role, that which is capable of making him holy. 'I will sing to my God so long as I live', says the Psalmist; and it is this celebration of God, of His perfections and His beauty that constitutes our chief glory. As Dylan Thomas wrote in a note to his *Collected Poems*, 'These poems, with all their crudities, doubts and confusions, are written for the love of Man and in praise of God'; and he added: 'and I'd be a damn' fool if they weren't', a 'damn' fool' certainly, if he wished his poetry to have anything more than an aesthetic appeal. But if as maker the artist actually makes his artwork, and if that work does possess a more-than-aesthetic quality—does possess a sacred quality—then is not the artist something more than a priest and does he not himself make something that is sacred? Does he not himself make things beautiful, divinize nature, and in the end is he not himself a power that sheds a divine and transforming illumination? As the young Gogol put it: 'If Art does not accomplish the miracle of transforming the soul of the spectator, it is but a transient passion . . ..'

Then, to add to the confusion, there is a great similarity between the aesthetic experience and the religious experience. Both can involve an attitude of contemplation, both may involve prayer and supplication. At its highest point, art aspires to a vision of the plenitude of being, to a vision of the world as it should be in its perfection. The true artist—I am speaking here only of the artist who does aspire to make his art a transforming power, to make the language of his art the signs of Paradise—will not see anything ugly in creation. Nor, bringing his light into the darkness, will he simply try to reproduce or copy what he sees. Rather he will try to see in all things their hidden beauty and to create in his art sensible forms which are receptacles of this ideal content. In this way he will give us his eyes so that we can in a fragment see the Whole that is present in it, like the sun reflected in a drop of water. Like a living being, the world turns towards us, speaks to us, confides to us its music, its hidden colours, fills us with uncontrollable joy and breaks through our isolation. We commune with the beauty of a landscape, of a face, of a poem, as we commune with a friend, and we feel a strange consonance with a reality that appears to be a portion of our own soul, lost and refound. Art 'dephenomalizes' ordinary reality and the whole world stands on the threshhold of mystery. Is not the art that achieves this a sacred art? Is not the artist who produces it at least a hierophant, a shower-forth of the sacred, if not in fact a maker of the sacred? Is not aesthetic practice, at this level, equivalent to religious practice?

We can only begin to answer these questions by trying to discern, however falteringly, what constitutes the line of demarcation between the aesthetic experience and the religious experience, and why a work of art which can bring us to the threshold of mystery is not the same as a sacred work of art, which discloses the mystery itself and makes us share in it. In other words, we have to discern what has to be presupposed before a work of art can be a sacred work of art.

The divine Logos, we said, is the underlying reality of things, their inner harmony; and this reality and harmony are present in all things however much they may be eclipsed and frustrated or abused and denied. We further said that the act of making sacred consists in a transfiguration of the object of the action, in the sense that this divine reality and harmony, immanent and potential in it, are realized in it and revealed to it. Its true nature is restored to it. It is delivered from its divided and alienated state, its state of estrangement from its true and intrinsic being, and restored to its permanent and uncreated state in the depths of divine life.

Such an action involves or, rather, presupposes a reciprocity of relationship, a reciprocal immanence, an inner congeneracy or likeness between God and the human and between the human and all other created things—a relationship, immanence and likeness entirely concealed from and even non-existent to the unregenerate consciousness and imagination. The bond uniting God and man, God and creation, without which nothing can be sacred, is necessarily hidden to and disregarded by such a consciousness and imagination, and the person who possesses them necessarily acts as though nothing is or can be sacred. The regenerate person, on the other hand, whose consciousness and imagination have been spiritualized, always tries to act as it were sacramentally, and he will move with reverance in the created world, seeing it illumined with the divine light that fills the sky, the earth and all that exists. He will venerate everything not on account of itself but because it is a receptacle of divine energy; and he will do this because he is aware that his failure to do so means that he is abusing and denigrating himself and as a consequence is abusing and denigrating everything else with which he comes into contact or makes use of because he is as totally unaware of its true nature as he is of his own true nature.

Since to restore or reveal this true nature to something is to bring it from darkness into light, and this light is the divine Logos—'I am the light of the world'—it is also and simultaneously to initiate it into the truth, goodness and beauty of its own being, for truth, goodness and beauty constitute the ultimate trinity of divine qualities. They are the distinguishing marks of the sacred. At the supreme summit of things, in their ultimate synthesis, the true and the good, in their symbiosis—their mutual interaction—give birth to beauty, are the source of beauty. 'Beauty is the splendour of the true', as Plato put it.

Yet at the same time beauty is an enigmatic quality, for if the truth is always beautiful, the beautiful is not always true. Its initial unity with truth and goodness can be disrupted. 'Beauty will save the world', said Dostoievsky, but he adds immediately afterwards: 'What beauty?' For, he says, 'The heart finds beauty even in shame, in the ideal of Sodom, which is that of the immense majority. It is the battle of the devil and God, and the human heart is the field of battle.' Plotinus is even more explicit: evil, he writes, 'is as though bound in beautiful fetters, as some prisoners are in chains of gold, and hidden by them, so that though it exists it may not be seen by the gods, and men may be able not always to look at evil, but even when they do look at it, may be accompanied by images of beauty . . ..'

It is not only God who can 'clothe Himself in beauty', evil can as well. The devil can transform himself into an angel of light. Indeed, is not beauty linked to the original fall of the most glorious of the angels? 'Thine heart was lifted up because of thy beauty, thou hast corrupted thy wisdom by reason of thy beauty.' (Ezekiel 29:17). Beauty placed beyond good and evil usurps the place of the Absolute, with total indifference towards truth and goodness; and it converts the human soul to its idolatrous cult. 'Alas, through the will of the devil who aspires to destroy the harmony of the universe, beauty has been thrown with terrible derisive laughter into an atrocious gulf,' wrote the sadder and wiser Gogol; as he also wrote, 'Better for you (Beauty) not to exist at all, to stay away from the world.'

This double-edged nature of beauty—reflected in the double-edged nature of art, whose most immediate and compelling touchstone is beauty—is due to the fact that though it is a divine quality it is also the supreme aesthetic value. It is its aesthetic value, not its divine quality, that the scholastics stress when they describe beauty as *id quod visum placet*, that which pleases when one sees it. For pleasure is symptomatic of aesthetic experience, of things sensibly perceived by means of artistic forms. The soul is not evil: it is by nature pure and immortal. But its vision can be obscured and vitiated; its organ of perception—the human imagination—can lose its contact with the divine imagination, to such an extent indeed that, as is only too clear from much contemporary art, forms and images which in themselves are sacred can be used in a manner that, far from nourishing, actively debases the mind and heart of those who come under their influence. And when the soul's vision and imagination are vitiated in this way, the soul's outlets on to the world of phenomena—the human senses—are also vitiated. 'Ears and eyes are bad witnesses for those with barbarian souls,' said Herakleitos.

When reduced to such an unnatural state the soul and the senses are incapable of perceiving or grasping the underlying reality of things, their sacred dimension or their hidden poetic essences, and these essences will always escape them. Consequently what the soul perceives when in this state it seeks to enter into communion with the world of phenomena will be not these phenomena in their own intrinsic identity, but simply reflections of itself projected into them, echoes of itself received back from them. It will as it were simply be disporting itself in its own waters, engaged in endless intercourse with itself; and the images engendered through this intercourse, androgynous and narcissistic, may well possess beauty, but this beauty will be but aesthetic or psychic, not sacred or spiritual.

It is because of this that if soul and senses are to perceive the spiritual beauty of things, their sacred dimension, an ascetic operation is required: a purification, a cleansing not so much of the gates of perception as of the soul itself. This could indeed be said to constitute another—the sixth—presupposition of the sacred, or of the actualization of the sacred. It is not that by means of this ascetic operation we have to suppress the senses, or that we have to replace them with another and new receptive organ. But they have to be restored to their natural state if through them we are to perceive what is beyond the senses, beyond the aesthetic as it is also beyond the psychic. And a precondition of this is that the soul itself has first to be restored to its natural state, to its original purity; and this means that the soul has to free itself from extraneous influences, from those images unleashed into it by its own aesthetic impulses, so that it may once more become receptive to the divine light and to the forms of eternal Wisdom which it communicates. Only in this light can it penetrate beyond the aesthetic experience of things and perceive their innermost reality, their sacredness. Only the spiritual can perceive the spiritual. And when the soul is restored in this way—made whole and sacred—and its imagination is regenerated, then the senses too are spiritualized, just as what they perceive is spiritualized: that which participates in the light itself becomes light.

This asceticism does not oppose the divine to the human, the supranatural to the natural. It is not a matter of transferring attention from a created 'object' to a divine 'object'. It is a matter of the metamorphosis or transformation of one's own subjective being. For only when such a transformation has been achieved in us are we in a position to distinguish between spiritual beauty and its aesthetic simulation, between the beauty that saves and the beauty that enslaves, because only then can we attune ourselves to and actively participate in the transfiguring beauty of the divine truth itself; only then can we see the beauty which is a transcendent quality of being, a quality of the divine light in which all things are made. Divine beauty, like this divine light, is neither material, nor sensible, nor of the imagination, nor intellectual; but it gives itself in itself or by means of the forms of this world and can be perceived equally well through the senses as through the intelligence and the imagination.

This is not a naturalistic mystique, nor a gross materialization of the spiritual. It is the vision, lived and experienced, of the communion of created nature in the uncreated reality of the Divine. It is in sanctity, in the Spirit, that man recovers the immediate intuition of true beauty. Salvation through beauty—the transfiguring of things through beauty—is not an autonomous principle of art. It is a religious affirmation. The beauty that saves—the beauty that consecrates the world and frees it from demonic possession—is a divine beauty, a quality totally rejected by the activities of the secular world and most of what passes for its art. For access to this beauty—the interior beauty, bearer of the sacred message—is barred by the angel with the flaming sword. The way to it is opened only by a birth in the Spirit—a rebirth—which is the death of art and its resurrection, its birth in an epiphanic art, an icon: in a recognition that true beauty resides not in nature as a self-subsistent reality but in the epiphany of the transcendent of which nature is the cosmic radiation, the cosmic manifestation and incarnation. The artist can achieve his true vocation—make his art a sacred art—only in a sacerdotal art, in accomplishing a theophanic sacrament and in bringing about what is to come: 'Behold, I make all things new'.

Here contemplation—not aesthetic but religious—reveals itself, in life as in art, as the loving of every created reality: a love, an 'ontological tenderness', that raises what is created above itself and liberates it from its bondage, its isolation, and even from death itself. Only in and through love is the ultimate innermost reality of things disclosed and fulfilled. Such love is not a divine quality, still less is it a personal attribute, something merely human and emotional. It is the is-ness of all divine qualities, their very essence. Apart from love there is no reason for the existence of the world—'God so loved the world'—and apart from love the world has no purpose in existing, all other purposes being either auxiliary or merely false and superfluous. It is the ultimate irreducible touchstone; it is the seal and the consummation of the sacred.

2

THE SACRAMENT

✠

The sacrament (*sacramentum*) is, etymologically, either a result of consecration or a means of consecrating by religious sanction.[1] The word began to be used in the Latin West in the third century as the equivalent of the Greek *mysterium*, which had the meaning of a reality that was hidden, or veiled, or kept secret, but was discovered or revealed or known through initiation (μυέω: I initiate). *Sacramentum* was a judicial term, belonging to the terminology of Roman jurisprudence, and is in a sense less adequate to convey the significance it is meant to indicate than the Greek *mysterium*. In early Christian language, *sacramentum* or *mysterium* was applied to any sacred action or object, in fact to anything which as mirror or form of the Divine was regarded as revealing the Divine. The number of 'mysteries' is therefore potentially limitless, for everything in the cosmos in some manner mirrors or enforms the Divine, and is thus a *mysterium*.

At the same time, there are particular *mysteria* of special significance in the mystagogic or liturgical life of the Church, the main two being the two evangelical mysteries of the Baptism and the Eucharist directly established by Christ. These particular *mysteria*, which include the whole liturgical life of the Church, came, by virtue of their special role in the Christian initiation, to occupy the status of what one might call the Greater Mysteries of the Church. From the historical point of view, it was only later that Christians began to reckon as the main mysteries of the Church the seven sacraments which nowadays people have in mind when they speak of the sacraments. But from a strictly doctrinal point of view, the number of sacraments cannot be fixed either at two or seven or indeed at any number at all, for the simple reason that, as is explained more fully below, the sacrament is not, and cannot be a part of, or included in, any quantity or quantitative reckoning: everything is capable of serving as the object of the sacrament, for everything is intrinsically consecrated and divine—is, in fact, intrinsically a *mysterium*.

This last remark, however, does not imply that it is meaningless to speak of particular mysteries, or of the Greater Mysteries, for the universal point of view embraces and does not exclude the individual point of view; and what is in question when speaking of particular or greater mysteries is not the intrinsic and essentially sacramental nature of everything *per se*, but a sacred hierarchy of mysteries established in view of the particular conditions of individual existence in the world. If one is to grasp the sacramental principle, one has to understand that these two ideas—first, that of the essentially (and thus equal) sacramental nature of everything and, second, that of a particular hierarchy of mysteries—do not contradict but, rather, complement one another. One must remember, too, that this is not an arbitrary distinction, but one imposed by the very nature of things, the whole created order being built up hierarchically, and yet all states in that order, whether individual or supra-individual, sensible or intelligible, being of equal significance with respect to the uncreated divine Essence. A failure to connect the universal with the individual point of view, as must be done if relative distinctions of this kind are to be synthesized and not taken as absolute, is always a sign that the full sacramental consciousness is being obscured by a too shallow approach to things.

Let us first consider the sacramental principle itself. It must at once, or once again, be stressed that the sacrament is not something set over against, or existing outside, the rest of life, so that it is sacred while the rest of life and all other things are non-sacred or profane or non-sacramental. It is not something extrinsic and fixed in its extrinsicality, as if by some sort of magical operation or *deus ex machina* the sacramental object is suddenly turned into something other than itself and different from all other created objects. On the contrary, what is indicated or revealed in the sacrament is something universal, the intrinsic sanctity and spirituality of all things, or what one might call their real nature. A recognition of the sacramental principle requires the recognition that nothing in life—in the created order—is, or can be, entirely profane or non-sacred; it requires the recognition of an essential likeness, a congeneracy or identity in difference, between the sanctifying power and what is sanctified, between the uncreated and the created; it requires, finally, the recognition that the sacrament has a cosmic significance and is intimately related to every single aspect of created existence, and that therefore, while the way of looking at or using created things may well be profane and non-sacred, the things themselves can never be.

This essential likeness or congeneracy between uncreated and created does not mean, however, that the object and action of the sacrament are a matter of indifference or that they can be indiscriminately exchanged. Every sacrament is absolutely unique in its significance; it is something which in spite or, rather, because of its universal nature, is singled out and set apart, inexchangeable and unrepeatable. How this is so can, perhaps, be explained as follows: while it is true that all created things are intrinsically sacramental and divine, it is also true that all creation is in a state of relative division, of relative separation and estrangement, from its intrinsic nature. It makes little difference whether one explains this in terms of a fall or of illusion or of a 'separation of the waters'; what is important is to recognize the fact (which is also in a sense illusory) of the relative division itself. All creation groans and travails for the revelation of the sons of light, all creation seeks deliverance, the world of sentient conditioned beings seeks deliverance. This antinomical character of creation (that on the one hand it is intrinsically divine, while on the other it is fallen, rent apart from the divine, and groans for deliverance) must be accepted if one is not to be led, or misled, into some kind of simplification or artificial solution, generally one that ignores the real suffering of all creatures.

From our point of view here, it is this antinomical character of creation that explains the significance of the sacramental object and act, and in what sense the sacrament, as well as being universal, is also unique and set apart. What distinguishes the sacrament and makes it unique and set apart is not that all creation is not intrinsically sacramental and divine (for unless all creation were intrinsically sacramental and divine there could be no sacrament at all): what, therefore, distinguishes and *makes necessary* the sacrament is not this, not creation's impotence or non-sacredness, but its divided state, its estrangement and alienation from its intrinsic nature. For in the sacrament this divided, estranged and alienated state of creation is transcended and its essential and intrinsic nature is revealed. To use familiar terms, the Divinity lies in all creatures in potentiality; if this Divinity were not immanent in all creatures, there could be no sacrament; there could, indeed, be no creatures.

At the same time, this intrinsically divine nature of creatures does not itself create a sacrament, for a sacrament implies a transfiguration of its object: in the sacrament, that is, God, immanent and potential in the creature, becomes active and is revealed. The sacrament is the anticipatory realization of the transfiguration, or the regeneration, of all creation. In it creation is delivered from its divided and alienated state and is established in its trans- or post-fallen state in the kingdom of God. That is why the sacrament is a matter of faith; of, that is, the eye of discrimination or eye of the heart which sees with a spiritual insight and is 'the substance of things hoped for, the evidence of things not seen'.

This antinomical character of creation explains, then, why the single sacramental act—each single realization of the essential and intrinsic nature of the creature, of the placing of the creature in God (where it is really what it is)—is both set apart and unique, and at the same time of a cosmic and universal significance. It is set apart and unique, as Christ, though a man among men, was also set apart and unique, because it must always happen in a particular time and place (in the tabernacle) in which a single fragment of creaturely existence is brought into the fullness of life and transcends its merely temporal and spatial limitations (though this transcending must not be confused with so-called other-worldliness, an attitude which is entirely non-sacramental). It is cosmic and universal because all life is one, and thus all creation is implicated in the realization of each single fragment of creaturely existence: 'Consider, O discerning man, that you are an image of God and the bond of all creation, both of the heavenly and of the terrestrial beings, and whenever you bend your head to worship and glorify God, all the creations, both heavenly and terrestrial, bow their heads with you and in you, to worship God; and whenever you do not worship and glorify Him, all the creations grieve over you and turn against you, and you fall from grace.'[2]

The sacrament is God's revelation of Himself to Himself in His creatures. Thus, in the sacrament it is always God who acts: the individual (the 'I' or ego) does nothing, is empty in kenotic self-sacrifice. In this sense the sacrament is the only true theurgy, a free breaking in of divine energy into cosmic life. As such, nothing can be equal to it and nothing can make it superfluous or replace it, for, simply, nothing can equal, make superfluous or replace God. It is because of this that no one can dispense with the sacrament (except in so far as he or she can dispense with God—i.e. cease to exist). The sacrament is God's supreme and original gift to man, to all creation, unique and universal. It is the original *Fiat lux*. That is why man, or any other creature, cannot possess or create the sacrament, whatever state of being he or it may occupy, for no man or any other creature, of however exalted a state, can possess or create God. Man, or any other creature, can only receive the sacrament, just as he or it can only receive God; though fully to understand what this sacramental giving and receiving implies is impossible for him who does not first realize that no one can give or receive anything, not even the most supreme gift of God, which he does not give to, or receive from, himself.

Here it is appropriate to point out something implicit in all that has been said above. Just as the full significance of the sacramental principle can only be grasped in the light of an understanding of the antinomical character of creation, so this latter understanding itself derives from an understanding of how God is both immanent in, and totally transcends, creation. Insistence on the total transcendence of the Divine, implying the illusory nature of created things, is obviously a denial of the whole sacramental principle (since there can be no sacrament unless the divine is immanent in the creature); insistence on the immanence of the Divine in such a way that created things are regarded as possessing reality in their own right, and not simply by derivation and participation, and that their utter dependence on the uncreated and transcendent is lost sight of, is again a denial of the whole sacramental principle (for if the Divine were immanent in this way creation would have no need of the sacrament and it would be superfluous). The sacramental consciousness requires the simultaneous recognition of both the total transcendence *and* the total immanence of the Divine, the affirmation of the one at the expense of the other being the negation of this consciousness and a major doctrinal error.

That is why also the sacramental consciousness implies a recognition of the Incarnation (in its cosmic as well as its historical sense), for each sacramental action and object *is* the incarnation, the unique giving of God in His totality to the creature, and the unique taking up of creaturely existence in its totality into the pre-existential uncreated divine Presence; it is the revelation to the creature, whatever its rank in the order of creation, of its permanent and uncreated state in the depth of divine life. Each sacrament in the full sense is thus the ending of self-division: the overcoming in the creature of that condition of estrangement and alienation from its true and intrinsic nature which marks its existence in the fallen world.

Having spoken in this way of the sacramental principle it may seem unnecessary to consider its application to the human individual. Nevertheless, the following may be said. First, whether the sacramental nature of a particular object or action is recognized depends not only on the object or action itself, but also on the attitude and approach—the state of consciousness—of the individual concerned in the recognition. As has been said, everything is intrinsically and potentially sacramental, and thus whether a particular individual realizes the sacramental nature of a particular object or action will depend on his own degree of realization. The sacrament involves or, rather, presupposes a reciprocity of relationship, a congeneracy or likeness, both between the Divine and the human, and between the human and other created states, that are by their nature concealed and unfathomable to the profane mind.

In a sense, how a human individual acts necessarily affects the whole of creation simply because the human individual is part of creation. Thus there is no escape for the human individual from a position of responsibility *vis à vis* the rest of creation. A failure to act sacramentally, or to recognize the sacrament, implies therefore first of all a failure to realize the presence, if only in a potential state, of the Divine in oneself and, second, and as a consequence, a failure to realize the presence, again if only in a potential state, of the Divine in other created things. As already observed, both the sacrament, and the bond uniting God and man, God and creation, are necessarily hidden and invisible to the unregenerate man, and such a man necessarily acts unsacramentally. Regenerate man, on the other hand, necessarily acts sacramentally, and his presence, and whatever he does, is a blessing to all creation. The saint is himself a sacrament, a living holocaust of divine energy.

Second, the question of the need for a particular hierarchy of sacraments divinely established with a view to individual salvation, and through which the individual may come to share actively in God's theurgic power, has been implicitly answered in what has already been said, especially in what has been said about the antinomical character of creation. All that might be added is that the purpose of the sacrament in this respect is to actualize or energize certain potentialities in the individual which otherwise are in danger of atrophy. It is to actualize and energize ultimately the divine image in the individual that otherwise lies dormant, passive and unrevealed. And another thing that might be added is that when man receives the gift of divine powers in the sacrament—a gift which makes it possible for him to transcend his fallen state and realize his divine potentialities—it is not only the particular individual that receives, but the whole of creation. Hence the sacrament is the most supreme act of compassion in which man can share.

Third, it may be asked whether, or to what extent, the Church's hierarchy of sacraments divinely established in view of individual (human and other) salvation may be affected by the loss of a true understanding of the nature of the sacrament on the part both of priests and people, a loss which, with the confusion of liturgical practice that often goes with it, might well be thought to prevent the transmission of divine powers through such sacraments. This is a question with many aspects, but in this context the following only need be said.

To begin with, how one considers the question (and even whether it has any sense) will depend almost entirely upon whether one accepts or rejects the sacramental principle itself. It must be repeated that the sacrament is not a piece of static ritual or sacred symbolism, still less is it a piece of machinery or magic or occultism: to regard it as any of these things is tantamount to regarding the *Fiat lux* or the Incarnation in the same way. The sacrament is the thing itself, reality itself, as it is in its naked essense and without anything being changed or symbolized or substituted. That is why a term like 'transubstantiation' tends to lead to confusion when applied to the sacrament, and generally indicates a certain failure to understand the sacramental principle: nothing is transubstantiated in the sacrament, for the simple reason that there is nothing to transubstantiate. The sacrament is a *transcensus* of the limitations of the fallen world, a recreation of the world 'as it was in the beginning'. Through it, its object is restored to its pre- or post-historical state of self-unity, to that state in which it is really what it is and always has been but which has been concealed beneath a veil of opacity and falsehood.

Thus there is in fact for one who has grasped the sacramental principle no question of whether the sacrament can be corrupted by the defamations of history, human aberration, the general confusion of forms, and so on, for the simple reason that the validity of the sacrament itself does not depend upon, and cannot be affected by, conditions of the merely historical, human, or created order. Neither history nor anything else can prevent things from being what they are, and neither history nor anything else can create or deform the sacrament, the very nature of which is uncreated and trans-historical.

Yet having said this it remains true that the sacrament, in so far as it is manifest in the liturgical life of the Church on earth, is, like the icon, only manifest under certain formal conditions; and if these formal conditions are lost or distorted, the living reality of the sacrament itself is eclipsed or distorted. And as for the icon, so for the sacrament the formal conditions of its manifestation are established by the canonic tradition of the Church. When the sacrament as celebrated in the local churches on earth is treated as a piece of static ritual or sacred symbolism; when it is regarded as an act performed by a priest before a more or less passive congregation whose co-operation is limited to a few responses; when the liturgical language itself has lost its creative or evocative power in the minds and hearts of the congregation; when the understanding of priests and laymen of the nature of the sacrament has fallen so low that it is imagined that the pronouncing by the priest of a few words of consecretation somehow turns the bread and the wine into the body and blood of Christ; when the whole business of church-going is no longer an inspired confrontation of man and his Maker in the fire of love and the Holy Spirit, but a dominantly social action or an investment in a policy for purely individual salvation decked out in the traditional trappings of religious forms which deaden rather than reveal the reality they are meant to express—when the sacrament is celebrated under such conditions as these one may doubt whether any effective transmission of divine powers takes place at all.

It is not that the sacrament ceases to be the sacrament. It is that its living reality is reduced to a state of potentiality where its participation by men and women is concerned. It is no longer active, no longer energized. The local churches themselves cease to be manifestations of the Church. The Church as presence and revelation on earth is also reduced to a potential state, its sacramental nature is hidden, obscured, inactive. The sacrament is rooted in divine theurgic life, the life of the Word or Logos in whom all things are made and who is in the world though the world knows Him not. Nothing of the world or of history can affect this. But when the world, and history, and man in the world and history, are divorced from and no longer share in the sacrament they are overcome by the sin of secularization and profanation, by the disintegration and evacuation of life. And this happens, both for the individual and for a community as a whole, when there is a loss of sacramental consciousness and of the formal conditions necessary for the manifestation of the sacrament on earth.

To say this is by no means to imply that this consciousness and these conditions are not any longer to be found in any local community of the Church, or that even, where they are lost, or appear to be lost, such loss or appearance of loss is either total or irrevocable. That is far from being the case. Indeed, to imply that such is now the situation would be tantamount to denying the reality of the sacramental principle itself, and thus to denying the reality of God Himself. The supreme sacrament is God. God and His Name are linked. Whoever forgets the Name of God, and does not recollect it and live in this sacred *anamnesis*, forgets God. This loss of memory is the loss of the sacramental consciousness. It is man's loss of himself. Whoever remembers the Name of God and lives and acts in continual *anamnesis* of it, lives and acts in God, and God lives and acts in him; and he too, and in him all creation, partake in the supreme sacrament, one with himself, in supreme Union.

NOTES

1 See E. Lampert, *The Divine Realm* (London, 1944), a book to which this chapter is greatly indebted.

2 Simon of Taibutheh. See 'Works of Simon Taibutheh' in *Woodbrook Studies*, Vol. VII, ed. etc, by A. Mingana (Cambridge, 1934), p. 23.

3

THE ARTIST AND THE SACRED: WHERE THE BATTLE LIES

✠

It is now more than a quarter of a century ago that the late Herbert Read published what were perhaps his final reflections on the state of the arts in the contemporary world. They were contained in an article to which he gave the title 'Testament' (see *Encounter*, October 1962). It is a striking and disquieting article, from many points of view. Read sees little hope for the arts. Indeed, he goes so far as to say that 'the arts fight a losing battle in our technological civilization.'. At the same time he insists that although the battle is being lost, or has in all but name already been lost, none the less artists must enlist in order to fight in it. Otherwise 'we retreat into despair, silence or some Dirt-dump'. At another point he is even more stringent: 'Every writer who retires to an Aegean Island . . . thereafter undergoes a subtle process of degeneration. It is not necessarily a physical degeneration . . . It is the workings of a remorse for the desertion of the front line of our fragmented and alienated societies.' Harsh words, especially to the ears of one who has 'retired' to an Aegean island; but not on that account necessarily untrue. What the article fails to say anything about, however, is why the arts are fighting a losing battle. And this, surely, is the crucial question, because until we have answered it we cannot really say who is fighting in the front line and who is not. We cannot even say where the front line is. That is why it is a question that every artist should try to answer; and what follows is my attempt to define briefly my position in relationship to it.

Whatever else one may say about works of art, it is quite clear that they are not self-generated or autonomous. They are born from or at least through living men and women. In this respect they take on the colour, if one may put it like this, of the people who give them birth. They reflect the way of life of these people, the state of their consciousness, the quality of their being. This way of life may be rich or poor, beautiful or ugly, significant or fatuous, human or inhuman: the works of art that come from it will be in the image of their particular parent. This is to say that works of art always follow, or derive from, the way of life (or state of consciousness, or quality of being) of those responsible for them. Living, or being, precedes its expression in artistic forms, and it is not the other way round. A spiritual or sacred art—the art, say, of Byzantium and of mediaeval Europe—presupposes a way of life centred in the knowledge and experience—or, rather, in a knowledge that is the experience—of spiritual realities. It presupposes a metaphysical view of the universe, one that sees reality as issuing from God in successive levels—levels that may be summarized as the spiritual, the psychic and the physical.

When this vision of things is lost, art ceases to have a spiritual or sacred content. This in its turn means that artists are no longer living a life in which the experience of spiritual realities is their overriding concern. It means that they are living a life in which either their individual psychic—and dominantly emotional—activities or their individual sense-reactions or a mixture of both are now the determinative factors. Correspondingly, they will see themselves and the world they live in as realities that exist in their own right apart from and independent of God. Western art of the last few centuries is for the most part a reflection of this way of looking at things. It is a record of what happens when man tries to live as though he were a self-subsistent being of psyche and sense and as though the universe is not multi-structured but to all intents and purposes limited to the purely psychological and physical dimensions.

A price has to be paid for everything: choice involves elimination. If I choose to live as though I were identified solely with my psychophysical aspects, or even if I choose to live as though I could be human while identifying solely with my psychophysical aspects, I eliminate from my life and hence from my art all that is more-than-psychophysical, all that is spiritual and capable of endowing myself and my art with a spiritual or sacred quality. I condemn myself to living in and creating a world which reflects more and more the idea that I now have of myself, the idea of what I now consider to be real and possible and important; which reflects more and more the norms of a profane outlook and the dominantly materialistic sense of life that goes with it. The final consequences of this choice, transposed to a communal scale and embracing for all effective purposes the whole of western society, is the modern technological world: a world which on the one hand represents the final objective embodiment of the norms of materialized reason and logic in its endless, annihilating, technical and mechanical processes and on the other hand is characterized by a blind search for ever more powerful, stimulating and violent forms of emotional or physical sensation. Such a world is indeed the *reductio ad absurdum* of a way of life based upon the notion that man is composed of soul and body and nothing more.

If in terms of this reading of our recent history we now ask why the arts are fighting a losing battle in our technological civilization or have already lost the battle, the answer will be similar to that given on another occasion—the devil cannot expel the devil. An art which is itself the product of exactly the same way of life or sense of life as that which has produced this civilization is powerless to prevent or check or in any way reorientate the development of the world of which it is a part: it is ultimately defeated from the start. Artists whose way of life does not include the experience of spiritual realities or even the acknowledgement of these realities, and whose art is therefore the product of their individual and subjective mental, emotional or sensational activities and preoccupations, are simply deluding themselves when they talk of being in the front line in a cultural battle against the domination of machines, the depravity of taste, the vast inhumanity that typify our contemporary societies: they are the servants and victims and instruments of exactly the influences that have shaped these societies, whatever gesture of defiance or cry of anger they may make against them.

For the bitter truth is that both the artists and the works of art that have formed the culture of our local European and American world—that culture for which Herbert Read told us we must fight—are for the most part among the chief agents of precisely that fragmentation and alienation the full effects of which are now all too evident. There can be no art that can resist, let alone prevent, the triumphal course of our technological civilization towards whatever nemesis it may be leading us except that which itself derives from a way of life whose vision and central experience transcend the categories, psychic and materialistic of which this civilization is the final monstrous projection. And there can be no art that manifests such vision and experience—no art that possesses a sacred quality—until there are artists who have first rediscovered how to live a way of life in which their realization is possible.

In short, the battle is not to be waged in the first instance on the so-called cultural front at all, and to act as though it were is inevitably to implicate oneself in and to implement the very process of degeneration that one most wishes to avoid. It may indeed be that the only positive course now available for the artist is one of retreat from the cultural battle, retreat not into despair or some dirt-dump but into silence or into what Yeats has called 'our proper dark', that chaos or abyss of pre-formal possibilities in which he may come to know the pre-artistic (because unmanifest) sources of spiritual energy from which our world is increasingly estranged. It may be that he has to renounce all art in the contemporary sense and to re-baptize himself in the waters of art's negation—waters that are the *fons et origo* of its existence. What, in other words, may be demanded is a renunciation as total as that of the catacombs and the monasteries, a renunciation from which sprang Aghia Sophia and Chartres, plainsong and icon, and through which was generated that spiritual capital of which the art and life of our post-mediaeval world have been first the exploitation, then the dissipation, and finally the exhaustion.

Yet even if such a renunciation is beyond his scope, he

must at least resign from the belief that with the weapons with which he is armed by our humanist and scientific culture he is capable of doing anything that doesn't make matters worse. He has to resign, not in the name of his civilization (by which in any case he has already been defeated, and in which in any case it is impossible to live creatively in the normal way), but in the name of those more-than-psychophysical, those spiritual realities that we have so neglected and denied. For unless he can do this—unless he can rediscover those realities and make them effective in his own life—he will not be able to confer on his art that more-than-psychophysical, that sacred quality which alone can help us towards the realization of values capable if not of displacing at least of indicting those that dominate our present desacralized world.

Yet given that an artist today would like to produce an art of this kind, is it possible for him to do so? Can he become so aware of spiritual realities that he is able to saturate his art with their lustre? An art that possesses a sacred quality is an art that mirrors the miraculous presence of the spiritual world. It is an echo from heaven on earth, transfiguring with a supranatural beauty the matter in which it is embodied, removing its opacity and making it a symbol of a higher level of reality. In this way it serves as a vehicle that puts man in mind of his spiritual origins and helps him in his efforts to return to them. It therefore presupposes on the part of the artist what we have called a metaphysical view of the universe, one that sees reality as issuing from God and as possessing a hierarchical—that is, a spiritual, psychic and material—structure. But it also presupposes the irruption of the higher level—the spiritual level—into the psychic and physical planes of his existence, for otherwise he cannot confer on the material of his art that luminosity without which it cannot properly be called sacred.

In a society in which a metaphysical view of things is the norm and whose members are all to a greater or lesser degree engaged in the practice of the religion in which this vision is enshrined and whose purpose is to awaken an awareness of it in every individual, it is quite clear how the artist can attain a personal experience of spiritual realities and so endow his art with a sacred quality. Moreover, the images and symbols of which he makes use in his art, as well as the method according to which he works, will for the most part be those already consecrated by his particular religion, and their efficacy in terms of producing a sacred art will already be well attested. In such a traditional society his art therefore will be to all intents and purposes a liturgical art, designed to function within a framework of worship and ritual observance, of prayer, ascetic practice and contemplation.

In our modern secular society none of this applies, and that is why the question of whether or not in its absence it is possible to produce an art that possesses a sacred quality is a very real one. It is easy to say that it is possible but only on condition that the artist affiliates himself to one of the traditional religions that still in spite of everything survives in the modern world, accepts its discipline, practices its spiritual exercises, and adopts its consecrated artistic forms and methods. But one wonders whether it is so simple. An artist must by definition make use of a language, pictorial, musical or verbal. If his art is to function, this language must be alive, dynamic, rooted in the artist's own experience and sensitivity. Moreover, it must be a language that communicates, if not to the whole of a given society, at least to those sections of it with which the artist in some way identifies himself. An artist cannot function in a vacuum, unrelated to a particular historical and social context. He must have one foot firmly in the world of time and place, in the world of change and transitoriness.

In a traditional society, this language is for the most part given to him. It is given to him in the forms and symbols of the religion that dominates his particular collectivity and marks all its activities. He will of course modify these forms and symbols according to his own particular sensibility and in response to certain inner needs of that collectivity in the time and place in which he lives. But any such modifications will be subordinate to the over-riding coherence of the traditional language of which he makes use—a language which he shares with his collectivity and through which consequently he can communicate in a living manner an awareness of spiritual realities to that collectivity.

In our society, an artist may still wish to communicate an awareness of spiritual realities, but the conditions under which he must do this have now radically changed. First of all, he will have no language which is given to him as it is in a traditional society. He must find his own language, his own voice. To say that he can find this language in the forms and symbols of the religion which his society has rejected, and so remind that society of them, is to ignore the other side of the artist's predicament: to be rooted in a particular historical and social context and to use a language that communicates vitally and dynamically to those to whom he tries to speak and for whom the language of a traditional religion has ceased to function creatively. For an artist to refuse to enter into the living actuality of his time and place, including all that is most sordid, tragic and wayward in them, or to refuse to speak in a language that reflects their temper and pathos, is for him to condemn his art to lifelessness and sterility.

This does not mean that the artist has to be politically committed. To discern where and in what forms the voice of eternity speaks in the broken accents of a disinherited time and place, and to give expression to this voice, demands a commitment, and a self-exposure, of a far deeper kind than that of mere politics. It demands an unflinching truth to one's own inner being and to the language that comes as genuinely, as non-artificially, from one's soul as the tree from the earth. In this respect it should be remembered that an artist is as much chosen as choosing: he is the messenger, the instrument—the victim even—of a power that he must obey as a condition of being an artist at all. This means among other things that a great deal of preparation for his work—its inner gestation and parturition—goes on at a level which he cannot consciously control, with the result that he cannot be precisely aware of the nature of what he is to produce or of the form it will have when produced, any more than a mother can be precisely aware of the nature of the child to which she is to give birth or of the form it will have. In this sense, an artist simply does what he has to do. To choose to do otherwise, however desirable for other external or objective reasons, is to cripple and defeat himself as an artist. This is to say, in this context, that it is impossible for an artist to continue to use a traditional language—in terms both of symbolism and method—when this has no vital creative link with his own world, inner or outer.

Indeed, part of the artist's task in communicating an awareness of spiritual realities in a secular society may require that he uses forms and methods that are specifically non-traditional in the liturgical sense, because only through such forms and methods may he be capable of transmitting to his spectators or readers or listeners a true and living awareness of what their life is like when reduced to a non-spiritual or non-traditional level. He may have to make them aware of the hell in which they live by projecting it before their consciousness in the forms of his art. In this way an art which appears to be the most anti-traditional in form and method may well have a sacred function or at least a sacred intention—T. S. Eliot's *The Waste Land* is a case in point. But this apart, the norms of a traditional liturgical art cannot serve to determine whether a work of art in a secular society has a sacred function or not.

In fact, it may not be going too far to claim that in a secular society an art which makes use of traditional forms and methods is likely to be a mere stereotype and not art at all in the creative sense of the word. Be this as it may, the art of a non-traditional society that seeks to communicate an awareness of spiritual realities, of the miraculous presence of the spiritual in the material, must do so in terms of symbols and images that will be but derivatively related to those of the liturgical art of a traditional society, or may not be related to them at all. In this respect it has to be remembered that as everything, rightly seen, mirrors the eternal, and as everything, rightly seen, is a symbol of a higher level of reality, a work of art may use a symbolism little related to that of a traditional liturgical art and may still act as a bridge between the material and the spiritual, earth and heaven, and may still possess a sacred quality and function.

This still leaves unanswered the question of how an artist in a society such as our own may himself become aware of spiritual realities and so be in a position to manifest them in his work. It may be taken as axiomatic that before he has given his assent to that metaphysical view of things of which I have spoken no artist is likely to embark on the task of trying to realize in terms of his own experience the possibilities it implies, still less to embody these in his art. But once he has given assent to it, it is certainly true that by affiliating himself to an authentic religious tradition, even if it is not one that commands the allegiance of the collectivity within which he lives, he may none the less by penetrating into its mysteries attain a spiritual awareness and so be able to infuse this awareness into the forms of his art.

Yet even without such affiliation an artist whose intention and attention is concentrated on the discovery and expression of spiritual principles within and without (and this, too, must presuppose his acceptance of a metaphysical view of the universe) may well be given moments of revelation and illumination, intimations and intuitions of eternity, and so transfigure the material of his art with that beauty and rhythm which are the hallmark of the sacred. To affirm this is not to propose, in a way that is now fashionable, that the artist enjoys some special status that exempts him from conditions that apply to 'ordinary' human beings, and so from the need to practise a spiritual discipline. Yet to deny it would be to deny not only the freedom of the Spirit to blow where He will* but also the testimony of those works of art produced during the last centuries—relatively few though they may be—that communicate such beauty and rhythm in spite of the fact that their creators have lived outside the framework of a formal religion. But whatever his course, of this the artist must be sure: that only when his art possesses a sacred quality will it present a positive challenge to our

* But see below, pp.132–3, for the significance of this biblical phrase.

technological world and to the degradation of human life which is endemic to it; and that he will be powerless to manifest such a quality in his art unless he has first made it effective in his own mind and heart. The primary battle is not cultural, but spiritual; and the artist has to fight it not in the thick of our fragmented and alienated society but in the depths of his own being, where alone its outcome will be decided.

4

MODERN ART AND THE HERESY OF HUMANISM

✠

I began the last chapter with a quotation from one of the later writings of Herbert Read (1893–1968). Read was a leading figure in the avant-garde of art, literature and aesthetics from the 1930s to the 1960s. Though he regarded himself primarily as a poet, in fact he devoted his main energies to exploring the meaning and significance of art and to making himself the apologist for modern art; and it is in this respect that he made his greatest contribution to the intellectual and cultural life of his times. Indeed, one can say that the scope of Read's influence is such that his ideas about art, its significance and function are those that still determine, consciously or unconsciously, the kind of mentality which is largely responsible for shaping contemporary aesthetic theory and practice. These ideas represent what may be taken to be the final flowering of the humanist phase of our culture, and it is because they continue to dominate the great majority of the modern art establishment, and hence the whole phenomenon of modern art, that they are of more than academic interest.

Read's thought begins to take shape in the years during and immediately subsequent to the First World War, when the erstwhile shades of Ruskin and Morris, Bergson and Croce, Hegel and Nietzsche preside over his meditations, while in the background hover the figures of Coleridge, Wordsworth and Goethe, strengthening that feeling for nature which he regarded as his birthright as the son of a Yorkshire yeoman farmer and which he never lost. From them, as well as from his reading of contemporary scientific works, he learnt above all to accept the concept which was to be axiomatic for him for the rest of his life: the concept that there is a natural evolutionary principle at work in all nature, just as there is in human life and consciousness. He never challenged this concept and it formed the cornerstone and key to all his subsequent thought. The counterpart to it was the idea of human perfectibility on the natural plane, if not now at least in the future: as Read began so he remained, a humanist, and he regarded humanism as 'the greatest exaltation of the mind of man that has ever been conceived'.

These basic notions survived even forty years of friendship and correspondence with T. S. Eliot, whom Read was first to meet in the early 20s, and from whose own thought Read's was increasingly to diverge. To what he regarded as an excessive importance attributed by Eliot to conscious, even rational, control in the production of a work of art, Read opposed a notion he borrowed initially from Bertrand Russell (though he found it confirmed in the works of T. E. Hulme, which he edited during this period), namely the notion of 'insight'—or 'instinct', or 'intuition'—as the first inkling of 'truth' in any process of apprehension, whether scientific or artistic. The corollary of this for Read was that the mind, given the raw material, works unconsciously to create. This led him directly to Freud and Jung, for in their concept of the unconscious he saw a possible source for the raw material of art as well as its shaping agent. From now on psychology—and in his later years almost exclusively Jungian psychology—was to provide a basis indispensable to his aesthetics. Indispensable too was the alliance of this aesthetics with modern scientific theory, exemplified for him above all in the works of Russell's collaborator, Alfred North Whitehead, although equally significant at a later date was D'Arcy Thompson's *On Growth and Form.* The best preparation, Read was to write, for a true appreciation of constructive art is a study of Whitehead.

Whitehead's philosophy, in common with much of Hulme's, was essentially Bergsonian, centering upon an evolutionary principle as the key to understanding the development of both mind and matter. Indeed, Bergson seemed to offer irrefutable arguments that consciousness, art and culture were evolving in time by processes comparable with those of natural evolution—that is, by proceeding from formlessness (the vast unconscious reservoir of insight or intuition) to ordered formation (the effect of giving form to the fleeting fragments of imagery gleaned by intuition from the unconscious). Such arguments provided Read with support for his notion of cultural progress and seemed to justify his belief in the vital role played by the avant-garde in art, by a vanguard of artists equipped with the only authentic kind of creativity. What Whitehead did for him was to redeem this evolutionary progress from a mechanistic or deterministic strait-jacket by introducing the conception of a discontinuous physics; for this notion of a quantum-leap in the progression from formlessness to form in the physical world could equally well be transferred to the field of artistic creation. Read now had a charter for what was to become a crucial theme of his aesthetics: that art was a natural organic process of unfolding, but not one whose forms could in any way be determined in advance. Hence the artist could be seen not simply as the passive recorder of a changing reality but as instrumental in the very process of evolution itself. In fact he played a central part in fulfilling what Read now recognized as the chief purpose of existence: the evolution of consciousness.

Over the course of time Read's thought was to seek new forms of expression, but his basic convictions, shaped above all by the influences we have noted, remained with him throughout his life. Art is unconscious expression, an organic event unfolding. By dipping deeply into his unconscious the artist may experience states of consciousness never before experienced and may have glimpses of the imagery through which this experience can be expressed. Increasingly for Read, the 'classic' idea of submitting the artist's findings to pre-existing forms of criteria became abhorrent and seen as a negation of true creativity. Such forms and criteria were associated entirely with convention and held to be irrelevant to the workings of a specifically modern creativity. Creative direction for the true artist was not to be determined by standards, intellectual or other, or by pre-set goals, or by prescribed compositional criteria. On the contrary, the main problem for the artist was how to free his mind from any reliance upon such conventional factors. Forms and images have to emerge spontaneously from the unconscious and any conscious control must by definition result in a deformation of the archetypal material presented by the unconscious, which is itself the exclusive forming principle. What the artist has to create is essentially a new reality: 'Only on that assumption', Read wrote, 'can we explain any form of evolutionary development in human consciousness . . .. An evolutionary advance emerges from the act of expression'.

Archetypal material, Read recognized, is indispensable, but it is ineffective if deliberately deployed. Hence less and less could Read accept that archetypes possess any formal coherence or any coherence that could be expressed only in a specific form or in a form already known. Rather archetypes are deep unconscious formless predispositions (but nothing more than predispositions) towards formal expression or symbolization, predispositions which have never previously been known or given any formal coherence. Thus when the artist by plunging into his unconscious encounters previously unknown states, his chief concern must be to allow the archetypal predisposition towards formal symbolization to express itself in its own way, which will be a completely new way. The forms of art are significant only in so far as they express such an archetypal predisposition. In some manner the imagery, however fragmentary it may be, that is latent in the archetypal predisposition condenses itself in the artist's unconscious into symbols. Art is this process of symbolic transformation and the authentic artist is one who has the power to symbolize archetypal feelings and intuitions in a previously unknown form.

What this symbolism signifies is, Read recognizes, totally unknown both to the artist and *a fortiori* to his public; and though it may subsequently become intelligible it will do so only by losing its dynamic creative potentiality and by degenerating into convention and cliché. Art, like life, has meaning, but a meaning never finally discoverable because of its continuous extension by the process of evolution.

Ultimately art is to be regarded as the symbolic form of a specific, extended or heightened inner experience, though whether this experience is archetypal or merely the secretion of a morbid or corrupt subjectivity gone haywire it is impossible to assess, for the simple reason that neither the artist nor his public possesses any criteria of discrimination according to which such an assessment can be made. One has in the end to accept the value of images and forms that appeal by virtue of an inexplicable sentience: the artist's task, faced by the unknown, is not to 'designate and signify' but to affirm unanalysed excitement. In extreme cases what his work may express is not so much the unconscious forces of the imagination as 'something as irresponsible as an angry gesture'.

With hindsight it is easy to see what could be—indeed, what inevitably would be—the consequences of accepting a theory of art and creativity such as this; and Read himself in his last years became increasingly alarmed and dismayed at what in all seriousness came to be promoted in its name as works of art in many leading galleries, not least of all at the Institute of Contemporary Arts, London, an institution which Read himself had been largely instrumental in founding. Yet, given the theory, it was difficult for him or for anyone else to adduce criteria according to which such works could be dismissed as the abortions and mockery they are, or to differentiate at all between the spurious and the authentic. The question which therefore arises is how could Read and all who shared and continue to share his views—perhaps the majority of the modern art world, critics and practitioners alike—have got into this kind of impasse.

The first thing to be said in this connection is that Read, during the whole span of his active career, was an atheist. He lost what religious faith he had at a relatively early age and, so one gathers, he never regained it. Consequently for him there was no ultimate reality, no complete truth, nothing of a trans-historical nature that had been given to man through revelation and could be known equally well at all times and in every place by those who took the trouble to know it. There was no spiritual world of living celestial beings or person-archetypes of whom every visible thing is in some manner an image and who constitute the celestial existence or essential identity of every created being. What modern science—including the science of psychology—took to be the real world he accepted as the real world.

One might say that this was Read's private affair and has nothing to do with his artistic theories which can be valid in their own right quite apart from whether or not he possessed personal beliefs of a religious nature. Unfortunately—or fortunately—it is not so simple. Art, like life, has one range of possibilities and purposes when you recognize and try to live in accordance with beliefs of a religious nature and quite another when you do not. Moreover, the choice is not between possessing beliefs or not possessing them but only between what kind of beliefs you hold. Belief, no less than air, is something from which man can exempt himself only on condition that he ceases to live and think. Thus if he does not recognize and accept beliefs of one pedigree and quality, he will recognize and accept those of another pedigree and quality, and they in their turn will determine what he regards as possible or impossible, true or false, real or unreal.

What does this mean in the context with which we are here concerned? If I recognize and attempt to live in accordance with beliefs of a religious nature I will also recognize and accept a body of doctrine in which these beliefs are enshrined. That is to say, I will accept *a priori* that there are certain realities to be known through the pursuit of my religion, that these realities embrace the plenitude of truth and beauty, that they have already been known and experienced countless times by the saints, sages and artists not only of my religion but possibly of other religions as well, and that only by attaining some personal knowledge and experience of them myself can I realize my own potentialities as a human being and bring my life to fruition. The corollary of this is that in so far as I fall short of attaining such knowledge and experience I am still imprisoned in a world of ignorance and illusion, exposed to demonic persuasion the identity of which I can recognize only because I accept 'on faith' the criteria of discrimination offered to me by the religion to which I subscribe.

If I am an artist my task defines itself correspondingly. I still accept *a priori* a doctrine of what is to be known and experienced, and I realize that my art will only be 'about anything', in the sense that it expresses what is real rather than unreal, genuine rather than spurious, on condition that it reflects or images—symbolizes with—the archetypal realities that constitute the essential identity of my own being as of every other form of life. This does not mean of course that I have to subject my imagination to a set of abstract concepts and rational propositions. Doctrine—religious doctrine—is not abstract or rational. It is symbolic and metaphorical. And what it symbolizes with or is a metaphor for are not abstract ideas or principles or laws but living beings. What is perceived on the horizon of the mental vision towards which religious doctrine reaches out and leads one are essentially personal figures or else relationships between them—relationships that are the ground of and that communicate their archetypal value to the earthly relationships that are patterned on them. If therefore my art is to express truth rather than falsehood, reality rather than unreality, I have to enter into direct personal relationship with the archetypal figure or figures with which the doctrine symbolizes and to communion with whom it has invited me.

This means that I have to realize as complete a self-identification as possible with the archetype. I have to eliminate from my mind the distracting influences of fugitive emotions and ego-sponsored images, all self-willing and self-thinking, and to allow the form of the person-archetype with whom my work of art is to symbolize to engender itself in my imagination, an act of visualization that itself draws this form into my imagination, ultimately from Heaven, immediately from the heart, the 'place' in which the only possible experience of reality is consummated. Such an act of visualization in the imagination is not the consequence of the projection into my psyche of fragmentary images of some state or archetypal predisposition previously unknown and never before experienced, and hence without any known and explicit doctrinal or formal equivalent. On the contrary, it is the outcome of the active and conscious engendering, in the imagination, of the forms that both correspond to what I already know is to be encountered and experienced and are capable of bringing this encountering and experiencing to fruition. Doctrine and art are thus complementary and interdependent: *Ars sine scientia nihil.*

Here too something else must be noted. We saw when speaking of Read's aesthetics that it became increasingly difficult for him to accept that archetypes possess any formal coherence or any coherence that can be expressed only in a specific form or in a form already known. Thus for him archetypes are essentially formless predispositions and nothing more. For the artist working within a religious perspective this is not the case. For him the archetypes are in full formal operation. This means that the forms and images of his art are not his own discovery or invention: they are pre-determined, both on the plane of the imagination and correspondingly in the given canonical prescriptions of his particular religious tradition. Again this does not signify that all an artist has to do is slavishly to copy the canonically prescribed forms: such a procedure would at once condemn his art to lifelessness and make it merely academic. If his art is to have life it must come from a union of his being with the being whose image his work is to enshrine, just as love can subsist only in the union of lover and beloved. But when a work of art is fully energized in this way—when theme and style are felt and lived—such categories as old and new are meaningless. What is important is not newness or innovation, still less any form of modernity, but the nowness—the immediacy—with which what is always to be expressed is expressed.

Thus there can be no such thing as an avant-garde among the artists of this kind of art, for the simple reason that there is nothing of which one can be *avant* or in the rear. Since this kind of art is the expression, not of a world of formlessness that for the first time is emerging into form, but of a continuous reality in full formal operation, the only ultimately valid questions to be asked when trying to assess the value of such a work are to what degree has the artist's imagination been informed by the archetypes of this reality and to what extent has he succeeded in communicating his apprehension of them in living terms. Moreover, though there may well be—in fact, inevitably will be—variations in the modes in which individual artists apprehend these archetypes, and so in some measure in their artistic styles, there is absolutely no value, and certainly no absolute value, to be attributed to the new or innovatory as such.

Concomitantly, in this perspective there can be no such thing as progress or evolution of consciousness in art, any more than there can be in life and culture as a whole, seen as taking place along the linear axis of the space-time continuum that we call history. Indeed, one would have thought that the absurdity of the very ideas of progress and evolution in this sense would be quite evident to anyone capable of responding even slightly to the great works of art which are part and parcel of our inheritance; for there is not and cannot be any criterion according to which it is possible to demonstrate that the artefacts of our modern civilization evince a higher degree of intelligence, beauty or of any other positive quality than, say, an Egyptian temple, the poetry of Homer and the Book of Kells. It would appear to follow that it is only in ignorance of man's artistic inheritance that one can seriously subscribe to ideas of this kind, an ignorance one might expect from scientists but not from those whose ostensible concern is with the arts themselves.

As for the purpose of such an art, this is what one might call liturgical, not simply in the sense that it serves man in his formal religious worship—though this may well be its highest function—but also in the sense that through it he 'celebrates the praises of the gods' in all his acts of making and doing, whether these be connected with the music and dance of his festivals or the patterning of the clothes he wears; for in this art beauty is never divorced from practical use or such use from the universal rhythm with which all life must be linked if it is not to lapse into disintegration and pointlessness. That is why ultimately the purpose of this art, whatever its form, is to help man to liberate himself from the world of illusion by offering to his contemplation images of a non-spurious reality; it is to bring the earthly and the celestial into conjunction, so that things may be seen not as they appear in themselves to our 'eyes of flesh' but more nearly as they are in God, or nearer to the source of their own being; it is, as Dante put it when speaking of the purpose of *La Divina Commedia,* 'to remove those living in this life from a state of misery and to bring them to a state of happiness', in other words, to facilitate the attainment by each individual of his own celestial existence, his own angelhood, by allowing him to perceive the difference between what he now is and what he has it in him to become, and by thus inviting him to achieve as full a realization of his being as is possible for him.

Such an understanding of the nature and purpose of art is immediately eclipsed in one who has no religious faith. It was eclipsed in Read. Nowhere in Thistlewood's book,* for instance, is there even a suggestion that for Read such an understanding might have some contemporary relevance. There is no reference whatsoever either to the art or to the artistic theories of Eric Gill or David Jones, all but Read's contemporaries and fully active both in producing works of art and in saying why they were producing them over the years in which Read was formulating his own theories. There is no mention of Jacques Maritain or of A. K. Coomaraswamy (though Read did once cross swords with the latter in the pages of the *Listener*). And if one asks why he could not envisage that such an understanding of art and its purpose might have some contemporary relevance, one can answer only by saying that, in the absence of a religious faith, he had to find other articles of faith, and those he found, and to which he gave his adherence, made it impossible for him to conceive that it could have any contemporary relevance.

As we have seen, the chief of these articles or tenets of faith that Read substituted for his loss of a religious faith was a belief in the reality of evolution. The theory of evolution—a hypothesis, like all other scientific theories—

is peculiar in that it implies an extreme, if often subtly concealed form of arrogance on the part of those who accept it. By accepting it one is committed also to accepting that theories or understandings held in the past are outmoded, however relevant they may have been in their own time, because human consciousness has now evolved or progressed beyond them. But this is only a covert—and not so covert—way of saying that one is more intelligent or in possession of a greater degree of knowledge than those of the past who formulated or adhered to such theories and understandings. A corollary of this is that one is further bound to assert that no degree of human consciousness or knowledge has been attained in the past which is higher or superior to that attained by the most advanced minds of one's own age. By the same token, failure to invent or subscribe to new theories and understandings, thus demonstrating that one is not in tune with the *zeitgeist* or with the new state of things now emerging for the first time into consciousness, is tantamount to confessing that one is stereotyped, hackneyed and virtually a museum-piece. One has, in Rimbaud's words, to be absolutely modern.

This among other things means one has to be a member of the avant-garde, that very special group of people probing forward into the unknown and gleaning from the formless depths of their unconscious fragmentary images of the future. Read himself was convinced that a number of special artists in his time—including Klee, Kandinsky, Mondrian, Gabo, Moore and Picasso—had thus shaped the foundation of a cultural regeneration. The new—that which is innovatory—becomes a value in its own right and there can by definition be no authentic creativity without innovation, either in style or theme but preferably in both. That it should manifest some heightened inner state of unanalysed excitement is all one can ultimately ask of a contemporary work of art, because there are not and there cannot be any criteria according to which one can evaluate or judge the irrelevance or relevance of the images and forms whose sole claim to be taken seriously is that they are expressing states of being and consciousness that have never been expressed or experienced before. This in effect is to deny that there can be any valid criticism of contemporary art at all, for if, as the theory asserts, you cannot know what the artist is intending to express in his work, clearly you are quite incapable of saying whether or not he has been successful in expressing it.

Such a conclusion is of course inherent in the premisses from which it develops: that man is no more than an inescapably time-bound, evolution-conditioned being with no immortal soul, and that his art and creativity cannot possess therefore any significance other than that which can be formulated quite adequately in hedonistic ('I know what I like'), sociological, scientific or psychological terms. Whether premisses and conclusion, as well as the kind of artefacts they foster, do justice to man, his creative spirit, or for that matter to anything else, is something which everyone has to decide for himself.

NOTE

1 See David Thistlewood, *Herbert Read: Formlessness and Form. An Introduction to his Aesthetics* (London, 1984), for a full account of Read's aesthetic theories.

5

ART AND ORIGINALITY

It is towards the end of his *Republic* that Plato introduces the discussion about art and artists, poetry and poets, in which he concludes that the artist is no fit candidate for admission to the well-ordered commonwealth. More often than not this conclusion is remembered while the argument on which it is based is forgotten. This argument presupposes that the universe is a hierarchic structure composed of different levels descending from the realm of intelligible Ideas or archetypes, and even from beyond that, down to the least particle of sensory or material existence. These levels are not separated from one another in such a way that each constitutes a self-contained and self-sufficient compartment. On the contrary, they all interconnect and inter-communicate, each level in the descending scale being the offspring of the one above it, while generating the one below it. There is thus an unbroken chain of subordination that from level to level gives coherence and unity to the universal hierarchy. Each level is in both a median and a mediating position; and all that distinguishes one level from the level above it is that it is more limited in scope, and so excludes certain of the qualities to be found in the level above it. Or at least it excludes these qualities in so far as they are less fully active and developed than in the level above; it does not exclude them as potentialities that it is capable of developing.

When it comes to considering those aspects of this hierarchic structure that we are able to experience through the senses, it may be said that every visible thing in our world has its origin in a corresponding invisible archetype that pre-exists on a higher level. It is a copy of this archetype, not simply a static or external copy, but one sharing a real affinity or kinship with its unseen original. Or it is an image of this archetype, in that it does not originate in itself or belong to itself but originates in the archetype of which it is the image and to which it owes absolutely everything it is. Reality, or greater reality, resides in the archetype. Whatever reality a thing possesses it derives from its archetype: it does not possess any intrinsic reality in its own right, as an autonomous entity. Compared with the reality of the archetype it is but a shadowy thing, and it will become still more a shadowy thing if it turns away from, or is persuaded to turn away from, its original. Conversely, if it moves towards its archetype by nourishing the potentialities that have been bestowed on it by the archetype, it will become less a shadowy thing, more imbued by those qualities—beauty, harmony, peace, being—that subsist in a fully developed and fully active state only in supreme reality itself.

The artist that Plato would exclude from his commonwealth is what we would call the naturalistic or realistic artist. He is the artist who takes as his model not the invisible archetypes but their multiple and fluctuating manifestations in the visible and material world, the world of change, as well as his own physical and psychological reactions to them. He thinks that in so doing he is representing reality whereas in fact he is but representing a reflection of reality. His art is therefore a reflection of a reflection, a copy of a copy, a shadow of a shadow. As such it can but lead people further away from reality, seduce them into the labyrinths of unreality, and confirm them in what is ultimately an illusion and a lie. Because Plato's concern is with truth and with true knowledge, he regards anything that contributes to confirming man in falsity and ignorance as unworthy of a place in the ideal human society; and as the art of the artists he has in mind does this, he would exclude such artists from his republic.

Yet the failure of these artists is not simply that they misrepresent reality. They also damage and corrupt the human soul. For just as the structure of reality is hierarchical, so for Plato is the structure of the human soul. In fact, Plato distinguishes three aspects of the soul. One is that according to which we are moved by our desire for something or, conversely, by our repulsion for it; the second is the highly charged emotive force that expresses itself in violent or vehement outbursts of feeling, chiefly feelings of anger; and the third is the power of the intelligence. The first two constitute what nowadays we would call the emotional side of our being, and indeed they do have this in common, that they are both brought into action under the stimulus of some external influence or object. They are, in other words, that part of our being which is acted upon and reacts to whatever it is that acts upon it.

The third aspect of the soul, the intelligence—which is by no means to be identified solely with the reason, since it possesses a capacity that goes far beyond ratiocination—is also its supreme aspect. It is the aspect that is capable of assessing and discriminating between the various influences and objects that affect the soul, of accepting those that accord with its knowledge of what is good and profitable, and of rejecting those that debase or are destructive. In this respect it is the active agent in the soul, that which is responsible for maintaining the soul's inner harmony and equilibrium, which it does by keeping control over the emotional aspects of our being, and by preventing them from reacting in ways that are discordant and uncoordinated. In a famous simile Plato likens the soul to the chariot drawn by two horses and driven by a single charioteer. The two horses correspond to the two emotional forces that he distinguishes, while the charioteer corresponds to the intelligence. So long as the charioteer holds the reins and guides the chariot in accordance with the principles of the supernal wisdom which he derives from his knowledge of the archetypes, all is well. But should he lose control, and should the horses pull the chariot this way and that as they react impulsively and indiscriminately to the multifarious disruptive influences that assault them from all sides, then they will drag the chariot—the soul—to destruction.

Yet it is precisely to the inferior, emotional aspects of the soul that the artist whom Plato would reject makes his appeal. As we saw, such an artist's attention is directed, not to the world of archetypes, but merely to their reflections in the material world; and his art is consequently but a reflection of these reflections, a copy of these copies. Hence it is capable of acting only upon the most exterior, excitable and fluctuating part of our being, persuading us to surrender ourselves to, and indulge ourselves in the various emotions and feelings it produces in us quite apart from whether or not these emotions and feelings conduce to the realization of the potentialities inherent in the higher part of our being, that which relates to the sphere of our intelligence and our spiritual nature. In other words, such art flatters and enforces our weaknesses, allowing us to attribute a spurious validity to their expression because we find them reflected, and so by implication validated, in the works that these poets and painters hold up for our admiration and enlightenment. Indeed, such artists are themselves under an impulsion to direct their art above all to the emotional side of our being, because if they are to have any popular success they cannot make it appeal too overtly to the intelligence: the lower emotional side of our nature is that which preponderates in most of us, while intelligence is cultivated and developed only by a few.

Hence these artists are unfit to be included in the Platonic commonwealth on two counts: first because their creations lack significance when assessed by the standards of truth and reality; and second because they make their appeal, not to the higher aspect of the soul, but to one which is as inferior as the world they represent. They are image-makers whose images are phantoms and shadows; and they seek to gratify the exterior or aesthetic aspects of our being. They deal with what is at third remove from reality, and they can produce their remote semblances with no knowledge of the truth. Living in a world of appearances, and adrift in a kind of twilight between reality and unreality, they reproduce only those vague penumbral notions that flatter the taste or evoke the applause of the ignorant and self-absorbed. As Plato himself puts it: 'Strip what the poet has to say of its poetical colouring, and reduce it to plain prose, and I think you know how little it amounts to. It is like a face lacking real beauty that has lost the bloom of youth.'

It is clear from what he writes elsewhere that Plato's

denigration of the artist applies not to every type of artist but only to the type that he is at pains to categorize in this particular discussion in the *Republic*. Nor from what is said in this discussion is it difficult to deduce the kind of artist from whom Plato would not withhold his approval. If what vitiates the art of the artist who mistakes the semblance for the reality is that by leading man away from reality it involves him even more deeply in illusions and unrealities which foster the baser aspects of his nature, then an art which does the opposite and directs attention to the truth must be ennobling and commendable. Such an art will be one that 'celebrates the praises of the gods', as Plato puts it. To celebrate the gods in this context means that the artist must give his attention, not to the appearances of reality or to his reactions to them, but to reality itself; not to the outward reflections, but to the inner and original archetypes or essences that animate and inspire them. The gods are these archetypes or essences. They are the ever-youthful, ever-productive sources of all that is revealed in the world of time and space.

By raising his intelligence—for they are intelligible realities—towards them and by apprehending or intuiting them in his inner vision, the artist will allow the radiations of their presence to flow into and to inform his work. At the same time his interpretation of human realities, of the mysteries of life and death, will be in the light of the understanding and criteria with which they provide him. His work will not then be at one with reality itself. But at least it will be an evocation or symbol of it, untrammelled as far as possible by his purely personal and private responses. As such it will be capable of reawakening in whoever approaches it a recollection of the reality that it evokes. It will not distract and disperse his attention among the ever-vanishing fugitive forms of the material world and his own emotional and psychological reactions to them. On the contrary, it will lead him back towards the ever-present and irrepressible life-giving springs which lie at the root of their as well as of his own existence. In this way it will be a means of helping to restore him to himself, of helping him to recover his true identity by liberating him from the false masks with which he is so desperately prone to confuse himself.

This of course is the nature and function of all sacred art and may even be said to be that which constitutes its sacredness. Indeed, it is only in the light of some such understanding of things as that which Plato proposes that we can begin to grasp certain features of traditions of sacred art—the art of ancient Egypt, the art of the Christian icon, the art of India and so on—that we tend to find daunting, not to say incomprehensible. The first such feature is the sheer persistence of these traditions. Conditioned as we are to expect and accept fashions and trends in art in which both the inner content and the outward form change virtually from generation to generation, if not from artist to artist, and which become dated almost as soon as the paint is dry on the canvas or the ink on the paper, it is bewildering for us to be confronted by an art whose form and content both remain, except for slight and sometimes imperceptible modifications, constant for anything up to two thousand years or more. Faced with this apparent enormity, we tend to seek refuge in some sociological explanation or other, such as that this art is one of the means by which a sacerdotal or royal caste attempts to ensure its continuation in power by maintaining a *status quo* in which a sacrosanct character is attributed to the role of priest or king. In so doing we both forget that no art can be produced under conditions of duress and reveal ourselves to be victims of exactly that kind of ignorance of which Plato accuses the artists whom he would refuse to admit to his republic.

For by definition a work of sacred art is the product of a vision that is concentrated on the inner essences or archetypes that lie behind and within the ever-changing world of physical and even psychological appearances; and as these essences and archetypes are themselves unchanging, their manifestation or expression in the forms of art will confer on that art a stability of content totally inaccessible to an art concerned primarily to represent the world of time and place and the artist's own emotional and psychological reactions to it. And once these forms themselves have been found adequate to the reality they aspire to enshrine, and so to fulfil their purpose or function of helping man to make or maintain contact with this reality (for such contact, however slight, is understood to be a condition of living a life not doomed to delinquency and disintegration), there is little point in deforming them in order to accommodate the whims and vagaries of the individual artist.

Naturally this art—a sacred art—makes its dominant appeal, not to our emotions, but to our intelligence; for the reality that it represents, whether in terms of sacred images or in terms of the human and other experience it interprets, is, as we said, an intelligible reality. It is this that explains how once we have learnt the symbolic language of one form of sacred art it becomes possible for us to learn the symbolic language of other such forms as well; for the reality that informs all such forms will ultimately be the same in each case, however much allowance has to be made for the different points of view from which it is approached. Consequently we simply have to apply the knowledge we have gained through our penetration into the inner content of one sacred form to the reading of another such form. On the other hand, for the person incapable of responding with his intelligence the symbols of every form of sacred art will remain a closed book, a dead language.

The second feature of traditions of sacred art that we tend to find baffling—and here we approach the main thrust of these considerations—is the capacity of this art to speak to us, once we have mastered its language, in a way that is limitlessly fresh and undated, whatever may be its age in terms of history or chronology. It possesses an immediacy and a contemporaneousness that we may look for in vain in works exhibited in our galleries of modern art or in anthologies of modern poetry, or indeed in much of the art of the post-Renaissance western world. Why this is so should not be too difficult for us to understand when once we have a clear idea of what is presupposed in the making of a work of sacred art. But for our immediate purpose—to explain why a work of sacred art possesses such a dateless quality—we can perhaps best achieve this clarification through an enquiry into what it is that constitutes true originality in a work of art.

When we call a work of art original or say that it possesses originality what we generally mean is that either it introduces some new and unfamiliar subject matter, or it involves new and unfamiliar techniques, or it does both. Innovation in one form or another is for us the hallmark of originality; and one of the factors, if not the main factor, that conduces to our calling someone an artist is that his work displays originality in this sense. Certainly at least it would be virtually impossible for us to apply this epithet to someone unless his work did display such originality. Failure to demonstrate innovation in one way or another would simply lead us to call the work academic, or derivative, or stereotyped, and its author a plagiarist or a mere copier, or something equally disparaging. A consequence of this is that everyone in our world who aspires to be an artist feels under a compulsion to be original, to express something new or to elaborate a new style or technique. We talk about a painter having to find his own style or a poet having to find his own voice. So great is the compulsion under which an aspiring artist works in this respect that almost by definition now he is forced to innovate before he can claim to be an artist at all.

In fact, of course, most such innovations are in the form of expression, in the elaboration and exploitation of new techniques, since even judged by present-day standards of what is new and what is not, originality in terms of content is beyond the capacity of most of us. In any case, the critics who establish the fashions in contemporary art would hardly presume to assess the value of a painting or a poem in terms of its content, first because what is being said is usually far from clear and second because to introduce value-judgments about a work of art on the basis of what it says, even when this is intelligible, would require a declaration of fundamental beliefs that very few critics other than avowed Marxist critics are willing to make. Hence, since *a priori* they demand that a work should display originality as a condition of qualifying in their eyes as a work of art at all, they are compelled to demand that it shows it in terms of stylistic or technical innovation. In this way they, too, aid and abet that endless pursuit of such innovation which characterizes so much of the artistic activity of our times.

There is no doubt an underlying logic in this pursuit of originality in terms of innovation, in this demand that every artist, in order to earn his title, must be original in this sense as though such originality were a positive, in fact an indispensable quality in its own right. It is a logic intimately intertwined with all our ideas about progress, evolution, extending the frontiers of knowledge, and so on, that are so much part and parcel of the modern scientific *weltanschauung* which still persists with us in spite of the indescribable mess into which it has led us. In fact, the emergence of these ideas is itself the direct consequence of displacing the mediaeval Christian vision which continued to see reality as a multi-levelled structure in terms very similar to those effective for the Platonic vision, and of gradually substituting for it the modern scientific outlook for which reality is reduced to a single time-space dimension and to the events that take place within it—that is to say, on the single material plane of what we call history; and it is as a result of this change of perspective that man's destiny is envisaged as attaining its fulfilment no longer in a transcendent, supra-historical state of being but in an ideal society towards which he is said to be advancing through time and which will be established in the purely historical future. This means that changes on the historical plane, the appearance, invention or discovery of what is new, begin to be credited with a positive value in their own right, for they are seen as the outward evidence of man's inner progress and evolution.

By the end of the nineteenth century such ideas as these had gained an overriding ascendancy; and it is in their light that we can understand why for an artist not to display originality in the sense we have been discussing would be little less than a confession of failure. For it would be tantamount to admitting that he is incapable of contributing anything to humanity's forward march, to the establishment of the *noosphere* (or whatever the term is that is now in favour when describing the future state towards which we are supposed to be advancing); and that due to this lack of genuine creative genius he is forced to resort to outmoded models, to the repetition of what has already been done or said by others, to be retrogressive, old-fashioned and out of touch, even guilty of putting the clock back.

Moreover, since our attention is now directed almost uncompromisingly towards the world of change, and such change by definition is endowed with a positive value because it is thought to be a condition of our evolution, and the manifest proof that we are in fact evolving, for an artist to opt out of this process and to refuse to show originality by not introducing into his work something that reflects this change, would be seen as a retrograde if not suicidal step, equivalent to that of a scientist who refused to make new experiments in order to advance the progress of his science. For an artist not to be original in the sense that we have been indicating would be for us, and for him, a contradiction in terms.

Originality where a work of sacred art is concerned has, on the other hand, a completely different meaning. Curiously enough, it is a meaning much more closely related to the etymology of the word. So far from denoting something novel in character and style, originality in a work of sacred art is the quality which relates that work to its origin, which relates it to its source or cause. For such a work to be original, therefore, it has to express or reveal such an origin; and what is meant when it is said that a work of sacred art possesses originality is not that there is something new about it but that it is a faithful image of an archetype. This archetype is the original which the sacred artist attempts to apprehend or intuit; and if his work possesses any originality it will be because he has to some degree been successful in this attempt and has therefore been able to inform his work with something of the substance of this original. In the case of such a work, therefore, originality has nothing to do with innovation either in terms of content or in terms of style or technique. It has to do simply with the fact that it symbolizes with or evokes the invisible reality of the archetype as faithfully as possible. It originates in this reality; and it is because it manifests its origin that it possesses originality.

We are now in a position to see why sacred art possesses such a trans-temporal capacity to communicate directly with our intelligence when once we have begun to master its symbolic language. It is that unlike non-sacred art, which attempts to represent the events of the ordinary everyday world and the feelings and ideas generated by our physical and psychological reactions to them, and so to express what is essentially subjective and transient, sacred art draws its sustenance, and its originality, from those ever-renewed and ever-renewing, inexhaustible and unfailing sources of life of which it is the image. It is their image not because it reflects them in an exterior and impersonal way but because there is a real sharing or participation of the image in the archetypal reality that is shown forth. The image is this archetypal reality in another mode. As such it embodies the actual presence of its original. There is a kind of equivalence or inner affinity between them. And this affinity or equivalence, which presupposes the actual presence of the archetype in the image, is not something that a work of sacred art can lose, or that can be withdrawn from it. It remains intrinsic to it, however long it may endure in terms of time. It can never become less original, less a contemporary expression of what always is, really and unchangeably, than it was when it first came into being.

The Indian dancer who dances a dance whose form was elaborated two thousand years ago or more is not merely repeating something that has been handed down to her from generation to generation and which still charms us because we still find the movements and gestures, the music and colour beautiful. She is actually revealing to us, and making present for us, something of the timeless inner and transcendent harmony and rhythm of life, as relevant, youthful, deathless and original today as it ever was or ever will be. No doubt she is able to do this because through long, patient and assiduous practice of, and spiritual meditation on, the form of the dance she herself has not only assimilated this form to such an extent that its transcendent supra-individual inspiration can flow through her unimpeded, but has also penetrated into its inner meaning in a way that implies that her own consciousness is now permeated by the higher consciousness her dance is to reveal. In a sense, it is no longer she who dances, it is the Lord of the dance who dances through her and in her. 'It is not I who live, but Christ in me', as St Paul expresses it in another context.

In this way her dance is truly a celebration of the praises of the gods, a celebration in which we too can participate provided we are willing and able to look on it not simply with what Blake would call our corporeal vision but also with the eyes of our intelligence. And this applies to all other types of sacred art: their originality remains always with them. And as they represent or show forth states of being or states of consciousness that correspond to permanent and ineradicable possibilities in our own nature, and so reveal to us what we could be if only we became what in the depths of ourselves we truly are, they retain always their capacity to promote within us, provided we learn to read their symbolic language with the eyes of the intelligence, that act of self-revelation and self-discovery which it is their proper function to initiate and to nourish.

Indeed, one begins to wonder whether our whole modern conception of the artist as a creative genius does not militate against or even effectively preclude the production of any works of art other than those that Plato would regard as unworthy of human attention. The artist who produces a work of sacred art could never think of himself as a creator or as a creative genius in the modern sense of the words, with all that they imply with regard to the originality of his work. The most he could think he could do would be to concreate. In fact, from our point of view what he does is more to reproduce than to create. He has to submit as though he had no higher aspiration and with a kind of obtuse compliance to the discipline of practising, through endless repetition, a given form until he has so mastered all its details that its original and transcendent inspiration can begin, as we said, to flow through him unimpeded and to animate his own workmanship. When this happens, when formal act and spiritual content begin to flow together, it will no longer be a matter of external copying or repetition; it will be a matter of directing the forces of inspiration of which he is now the vehicle into formal patterns that long practice and meditation have enabled him to master, inwardly and outwardly. In doing this, his effort will be to exclude all originality in the modern sense. In fact his whole undertaking requires an increasing self-effacement, an increasing liberation from all desire for self-expression, or for the expression of his own genius and individuality. So much is this the case that he may not even permit his name to be attached to his work, since the mere fact of claiming it as his own work would be for him proof that he has not yet attained, as man and artist, the degree of perfection—of true originality, or return to the origin—to which he is summoned.

It will be clear from this that such self-effacement is not in the least something negative. On the contrary, it is a condition of the artist's realization of his status as the mediator between higher and lower levels of reality, of his sense of responsibility as a catalyst through whose agency his fellow-beings may be reminded or made mindful of their own origins, so eclipsed by their attachment to the shadow-world of the empirical ego. For such realization presupposes that the artist frees his own consciousness from this attachment and raises it to the level in which the archetype of his own true being exercises its transfiguring and liberating power. It is knowledge of the world of the archetypes which the artist attains through the realization of his own true being that in its turn permits him to infuse into the forms of his art a similar power. In this way he participates by means of his art in the whole theurgic process on which the equilibrium and harmony of the universe depends, level mirroring level, intelligible and sensible linked in profound communion. His role is thus a priest-like one in that he becomes an instrument through which the higher performs with respect to the lower a function that is at once both revelatory and redemptive.

All this is very far from what tends to be the attitude and practice of the modern artist, especially when, as is so often the case, he does not even acknowledge supernal realities, let alone try to celebrate them in his work. And if this does imply that such an artist is thereby precluded from producing a work which has the quality and function that give sacred art such a crucial role wherever and whenever it is recognized, should we not ask him, and ourselves, what claim his art has to our attention and of what significance is the self-determined originality that he feels under such an obligation to display?

6

THE ART OF THE ICON

✠

The icon, as the sacred art *par excellence* of the Orthodox Christian tradition, attained its mature form during the Byzantine period. When in the first half of the fourth century AD, Constantine the Great, now sole ruler of the Roman Empire, established his new capital at Byzantium, a town at the junction of the Sea of Marmara and the Bosphorus, he shifted the cultural axis of the Empire from the Roman to the Greek-Anatolian world; at the same time, by himself embracing Christianity, he initiated the gradual conversion of the Roman Empire into the East Christian Empire. It is from these two events, with all their implications, that the art of the icon developed. Christians of course already had their own art before this. Chiefly it was the art of the catacombs at Rome and at one or two other places, and of the reliefs decorating sarcophagi found in Italy and southern Gaul; while in the East there are the paintings in a small private baptistery at Dura Europos on the Euphrates, dating from the early years of the third century.

Yet in one sense this early Christian art can hardly be called specifically Christian at all. For, to start with, it has no specifically religious or Christian content. Where its form is concerned, this is the same as that of contemporary products from non-Christian workshops, whether these were intended for cult purposes or simply for decoration; and where its subjects are concerned, these are drawn, with slight adaptations to suit their new Christian setting, from the vast storehouse of classical tradition: Christ as the Good Shepherd derives from Hermes Criophoros, Jonah asleep under his gourd is the sleeping Endymion; and whole mythological themes, such as those connected with Orpheus, Psyche and Eros, are taken over entire, the only change being the message they are intended to convey. This early Christian art is indeed really a language of signs: it is meant to point the way to the Christian mystery, to the mystery of deliverance from death and sin through the sacraments of Baptism and the Eucharist. It is not either descriptive or expressive; there are no individualized saintly figures or real evocations of sacred themes. In its chaste, self-denying abruptness, early Christian art seems almost a renunciation of art.

With the conversion of Constantine and the subsequent christianization of the Empire, Christian art came out of the catacombs. It became public. It became even the official art of the imperial administration. The secret mystery, reserved for Christian initiates alone, now became a liturgy that must be proclaimed to all. In the meantime, the early Fathers of the Church were formulating in precise intellectual terms some of the fundamental truths of the Christian religion. A whole cosmology with its sacred figures and its mythological scenes was waiting to be given artistic shape. For this purpose the simplified, almost impressionistic technique of early Christian art was inadequate. Richer, more elaborate forms were needed.

Models for the portraiture of saintly figures were to be found in the secular funerary portraits of the non-Christian period, especially those in Roman Egypt—the Fayum portraiture with the solemn staring eyes, thick eyebrows and dark-lined noses. The earliest examples of Christian portraiture deriving from these models are of the full-faced and motionless heads painted in encaustic wax on wooden tablets, now in the monastery of St Catherine on Mount Sinai, and dating from the fifth century. In the West, at Ravenna, the imperial mosaic portraiture of the Emperor Justinian and the Empress Theodora with their attendants at the church of San Vitale (sixth century), and the long friezes of male and female saints in the nearby church of Sant' Apollinare, are in a similar style.

For the depiction of larger sacred scenes, biblical or other, requiring a landscape or other natural features, the Christian artist could draw on the whole tradition of landscape painting in Roman and Hellenistic art. This art provided the

East Christian Empire with an immense reserve of natural observations transposed into a clearly defined pictorial language of an extreme delicacy and lyricism. Orthodox Christian artists assimilated this language, as they assimilated the Fayum portraiture, but gave both a new depth, a new inwardness, in accordance with their new spiritual purpose. For it must be remembered that Orthodox Christian art is no mere development of past tastes and styles, whatever these may have been, and however greatly it may have borrowed from them. In fact, its roots do not lie in art at all. They lie in the spiritual realities at the heart of the Christian faith.

Here precisely we are likely to run into danger, for during the last few decades this art—the art of the icon—seems to have come into fashion. It is no longer abused for its lack of perspective, nor are its artists for their ignorance of human anatomy. Now on the contrary it is acclaimed as one of the significant art forms of the European spirit. This may all be to the good. It may be to our credit that we now recognize the icon as respectable and authentic. But there is a danger involved. There is a danger that in its new found popularity its proper nature may be submerged and lost. We may forget that if the icon is a work of art, it is a work of art with a difference and that if we ignore this difference we are in danger of regarding the icon not as what it is, but according to the vagaries of our own taste and appreciation.

Indeed, one may suspect that this has already happened to quite a large extent: the icon has become respectable, a fit theme for academic discourse or museum display, a commercial commodity, if not entirely at least partly because we are no longer fully aware of what it is. As art critics and art historians we treat it as we would treat other works of art. We discuss it from the aesthetic point of view, as we would a picture by Rembrandt or Picasso. We try to find out the date at which a certain icon was painted. We seek to attribute it to a particular iconographer, or to a particular school of iconographers. We note stylistic influences, trace stylistic sequences. We label it Byzantine art or art in the Byzantine style, in the way that we might label other works Renaissance art, or Baroque art, in order to place them within a period, to fit them into our perspective of the past or into the appropriate part of a museum or art gallery.

There may be no particular harm in this, just as there may be no particular harm in the satisfaction of various other human foibles. But if we think that by doing all this we are getting to know more about the icon we are mistaken. For where the icon is concerned or, rather, where the understanding of the art and function of the icon is concerned, all this—dating, attributions, schools, influences, stylistic sequences: the normal pursuits of art critics and historians—is, or may be, interesting, but it is not entirely to the point.

To start with, if the icon is a work of art, it is not one which is similar in kind to other works of art. It is not even a work of religious art, as we have come to use the term. What we tend to call a work of religious art is a work with a religious theme. If it is of the Christian tradition that we are speaking, then a work of religious art is a work which presents to our view scenes drawn from the scriptures or from the lives of the saints or from some other recognized source. Because an icon also presents such a subject, we classify it too as religious, as we do a picture of the holy family by Raphael or of the Crucifixion by Matisse. In so doing we forget that what determines the nature of a work of art is not so much its subject as its form; and that while a work of art may be called religious because its subject is drawn from the storehouse of scriptural text or sacred legend, it cannot be called an icon unless its form derives from spiritual vision, spiritual understanding, and is fused (though not confused) with this spiritual content. In other words the icon is, as we said, a work of sacred art—the major, if not the sole, pictorial form of sacred art in the Christian tradition.

This leads to the second thing that has to be said about the icon. An icon is not something which can be regarded as a self-contained whole, complete in itself. We have become accustomed to looking at works of art as independent entities, areas of line and colour cut off from surrounding space, enclosed in a frame and hung up on a wall. The icon is not like this. It cannot be separated off in this fashion. On the contrary, it is something whose full nature cannot be understood unless it is seen in relationship to the organic whole of the spiritual structure of which it forms a part. Divorced from this whole, hung in a frame upon a wall, and looked at as an individual aesthetic object, it is divorced from the context in which it can function as an icon. It may then be an attractive piece of decoration, but as an icon it ceases to exist. For as an icon it can exist only within the particular framework of belief and worship to which it belongs. Divorced from this framework it ceases to be an icon. It becomes a contradiction in terms. For an icon is not only a work of sacred art; it is also a work of liturgical art.

It could of course be said that any work of sacred art is by definition also a work of liturgical art. It is inconceivable for a work of sacred art not to belong to a framework of belief and worship, for a work of sacred art presupposes the context of a spiritual tradition, and a spiritual tradition in its turn necessarily embraces such a structure. What distinguishes the icon as a work of sacred art is that it presupposes the context of the Christian tradition and that the framework of belief and worship to which it belongs is the Christian liturgy. As what this means in concrete terms is now unfamiliar to a world in which the norms of sacred art not only as a whole but even where the Christian tradition is concerned are virtually unknown and ineffective, something must be said by way of clarification if the proper significance and role of the icon is to be understood. This, *mutatis mutandis,* will also clarify the significance and role of every form of sacred art.

To affirm that the framework of belief and worship to which the icon belongs is the Christian liturgy is to say that it is part and parcel of a visual system conveying and giving support to the spiritual facts or spiritual events that underlie the whole drama of this liturgy. It follows from this that if we are to have some understanding of the icon we must first have some understanding of the spiritual facts or events underlying the liturgy of which it constitutes an aspect. This does not mean that we have to enter into any long theological discussion; but a few words must be said to indicate the nature of the Christian liturgy, so that we can then see what is meant by saying that the icon is a form of liturgical art.

The liturgy is something like a mystery play or an ancient Greek drama which leads the spectator stage by stage and act by act towards its climax. In this case the climax is represented by the central Christian mystery, the sacrament of the Eucharist, in which the worshipper is also asked to participate. The liturgy, then, is designed to lead the worshipper towards this participation in the sacrament. The various stages and acts of the liturgy, the various liturgical forms, are means to this end. They act as a preparation for the approach to the central mystery. They prepare the psychological ground, so that the worshipper shall be in the right frame of mind when the climax of the liturgy is reached.

What in fact has to be conveyed to the worshipper if he is to be in this right frame of mind? The answer to this is that what has to be conveyed is a sense of the reality of those two main events of which the sacrament of the Eucharist is the consummation. These two main events are the Incarnation and the Transfiguration. They are indeed what one might call the two poles of the whole Christian scheme of salvation. The one pole—the Incarnation—signifies the actualization of the Spirit in matter, in human and natural existence. The other pole—the Transfiguration—makes evident the consequence of this, and that is the sanctification or spiritualization of matter and of human and natural existence. 'God became man so that man might become God' is the traditional patristic formula in which this scheme of salvation is expressed.

The Eucharist imitates and repeats this scheme. In it the Spirit, passively present in the elements of bread and wine, becomes active in and sanctifies them, filling the elements with divine grace. In this way the Eucharist is the means through which God's redemptive and transfiguring activity continues through time. It is an image of the Saviour, an image of mercy that is able to bring about the salvation of man. An image, it should be repeated at this point, is not simply a sign for something. It does not simply indicate something other than itself, as smoke may indicate fire, or as a cry may indicate pain. On the contrary, an image shares in the nature of the object of which it is an image, there is an actual presence of the one in the other, a physical fusion (though again not confusion), so that knowing the image we are in the same instant made aware of the object which it reveals. And this is to say that an image does not, as a sign, merely indicate; it also brings about the effect it indicates; it compels us, to the degree to which we submit or are receptive to its influence, actually to experience that life which it mysteriously mirrors and enshrines. And it is in this sense that the Eucharist is an image: it is an instrument charged with the divine which has the power to confer an inner sanctity on whoever moves towards it.

It can now be understood what is meant by saying that the icon is a liturgical art: it is one of the means through which the sense of the reality of the Incarnation and the Transfiguration is conveyed to the worshipper, one of the means therefore through which the worshipper is put into the right frame of mind for that climax of the liturgical drama which is the sacrament of the Eucharist. If the Eucharist is the image of the Christian Saviour, the divine master-work, then the icon in its turn is an image of the Eucharist, leading the mind directly to the Eucharist, to the heart of the Christian mystery. For the icon testifies to the basic realities of the Christian faith—to the reality of the divine penetration of the human and natural world, and to the reality of that sanctification which results from this. And as these two basic realities also contain and imply a whole cosmology, the icon also testifies to the Christian scheme of the universe, to the Christian world-picture.

The icon is not an imitation of the natural world, a copy of natural models. It does not enter into competition with the unattainable perfection of the world, as classical art, for instance, so often tries to do; nor does it aspire, again as classical art so often does, to a serenity in terms of this world—an aspiration which, because of its impossibility, results in a falsifying idealism. On the contrary, the icon seeks to express a structure of ideas. It seeks to convey to us a picture of the divine world order—that is, a picture of how things are in their true state, or in 'the eyes of God', and not at they appear to us from our limited point of view.

This can most clearly be seen in the fully developed iconographic scheme of the Christian church. The church is itself an image of the universe—an icon of the universe according to the Christian pattern. According to this pattern, the universe is built up on a hierarchic scale of different levels of being, each issuing from and depending on the one above it. This scale is often regarded as threefold. The highest level of the scale is the heavenly and uncreated world of divine being; the next level corresponds to the world of Paradise, to the world as it was created 'in the beginning'—a world which was deformed through the fall of man, and was reformed through the Incarnation and the whole cycle of events which make up the life of Christ, or the New Testament. The third level is that of human and terrestrial existence, of this existence not in its fallen state but in the process of that deification through the activity of the Holy Spirit by which it comes to realize the state of human nature recreated by the Saviour.

These three levels can be clearly distinguished in the iconographic (and architectural) scheme of the church. First, there is the divine world shown forth in the dome and on the high vaults; second, on the squinches, the pendentives, the upper parts of the walls are scenes dedicated to the life of Christ, to that recreating of human and other nature, and to the regaining of Paradise in the heavenly Jerusalem; third, on the lower or secondary vaults and on the lower walls are images of the saints and martyrs, holy men and women who already have a part in the redeemed world. In this way, on entering the church the worshipper has before him a whole picture of the universe, hierarchically graded according to the degree of being possessed by the various figures occupying the different levels.

Thus, in the dome there is the figure of the Son of God, the Logos or Divine Word, who is not only Being itself, but also the source of being for all lower levels. He is the All-ruler, the Pantocrator and the Creator. He occupies the centre of the dome, the centre of the heavens and of the universe. Below and round him radiate like spokes of a wheel various spiritual powers, archangels or angels, sometimes apostles or prophets. These are as it were intermediaries between the uncreated divine world and the created world. Also, in relation to the liturgy, which is our concern here, they are announcers and mediators of the Incarnation, of the descent of the Son of God to earth.

The events of this descent are figured below these, in the second zone, in the secondary vaults and on the straight walls. Here are depicted scenes from Christ's life on earth. These comprise, in their classical form, the twelve main feasts of the Christian year: the Annunciation, the Nativity, the Presentation in the Temple, the Baptism, the Transfiguration, the Raising of Lazarus, the Entry into Jerusalem, the Crucifixion, and Anastasis (Descent into Hades), the Ascension, the Pentecost and the Koimisis (the Dormition of the Virgin). These correspond to the various stages of the scheme of salvation—they are reminders of the way to be followed in the return to Paradise.

Beneath these again are standing figures of saints and martyrs, the holy men and women who have already followed that way of return. They testify not only to the reality of the Incarnation, but also to the reality of that sanctification in the Spirit which consummates the purpose of the Incarnation. These portraits are not portraits of men and women in their fallen state. They are portraits of a deified humanity, of men and women who have cleansed the divine image in themselves which had been obscured and troubled by the fall, and who participate in the here and now of the new heaven and the new earth. What they show forth is the state of being which it is, or should be, the worshipper's desire to achieve through his initiation into the Christian mystery. Once again the connection with the liturgy is obvious and intimate.

Below these, on the floor of the church, is the congregation—the congregation of those who have entered on the way of salvation and are aspiring towards those levels of being which they see imaged on the walls around them.

They are between outer darkness—the world outside the Church—and the Kingdom of God, the New Jerusalem which is revealed to their inner eye through its projection in visible terms into the space of the church.

It must be remembered in this connection that these various levels and states of being mirrored in the space of the church are not, according to Christian understanding, merely outside man; they are also within him. The church, that is, with its iconographic scheme, is not merely a diagram in miniature of the universe; it is also a diagram of man's inner world. According to the Christian view of things, man is the mirror of the universe—or, rather, in man are present, in a passive if not in an active mode, all those levels of being that constitute the universe. Thus, in his spiritual intelligence, man is in the image of God; in his soul, he embraces the angelic world of the imagination and of thought, while in his body he is linked to the physical world. In this way he holds a middle position between the higher and lower levels of creation. In his triple nature of spirit, soul, and body he unites these higher and lower levels. This position of man constitutes his dignity and it makes him not only superior to the animals but also to the angels, since he is more inclusive than an angel.

Usually, though, and abnormally, he behaves and regards himself as though he were made up only of the lower levels of his nature—as though he were only a creature of soul and body—and he forgets about his higher levels, his spiritual nature. He forgets his true dignity. The iconic forms of the church are thus reminders to him of what this dignity is. They show him what he is in reality—or what from his immediate point of view he is capable of becoming: a dweller in eternity, a sharer of angelic life, as well as an earth-bound creature of time. If he were but capable of mobilizing, of bringing into play the higher levels of his being which he sees reflected in the icons about him, he would then be capable of occupying the position for which he was originally created.

It is this bringing into play of these higher levels of being that is the intention of the Eucharist. And here another aspect of the iconographic scheme of the church is evident.

We have already glanced at what we might call the spatial aspect of this scheme—the icons of the various levels of being descending in a hierarchic fashion from the divine level in the dome down to the human level standing on the floor of the church: descending from the world of eternity to the world of time. Now we must glance at what we might call the temporal aspect of the scheme—that is, at how the iconography supports the idea or conveys the reality of the continuing nature of the divine activity in the eucharistic sacrament.

Here the centre of attention is of course the sanctuary. This is separated off from the main body of the church and thus from the congregation by a screen, the iconostasion, which itself bears icons, the main two being those of Christ and Mary, on either side of the royal doors. This screen indicates the limit separating the world of sense from the spiritual world, and it is for this reason that the icons appear at this point, as uniting the two worlds, as the world of the imagination in man stands between his spiritual nature and his sensory faculties. Beyond the screen is the sanctuary, the holy of holies or the divine dwelling place. It is here that the sacrament of the Eucharist is celebrated and hence the images which surround it express the whole economy of the sacrament in a still more direct way than those in other parts of the church.

It must be remembered that according to Christian understanding it is Christ himself who is invisibly present in the visible form of the sacrament; and this too is shown forth in the icons depicted around the altar. Here Christ is shown as the sacrificer and what is sacrificed, offerer and offered, priest and oblation. Then, as we said, the Eucharist, being the image of the Saviour, is also an imitation of the Incarnation. Thus in order for it to be accomplished there must be an imitation of all those divine-human events of which the prototypes are revealed in the Gospel narrative of the birth of Christ. There must be, that is, a birth of the Logos in matter, in the human and natural world, a 'taking of flesh' ἐκ Πνεύματος Ἁγίου καὶ Μαρίας τῆς Παρθένου—of the Holy Spirit and of Mary the Virgin. That is why above the altar—which symbolically is the place of the divine birth, the image of Bethlehem—is the icon of the Mother of God.

For the Mother of God stands also between the divine and the human worlds, between the higher uncreated levels of being and the lower created levels: she mediates between these worlds, receiving the Spirit 'from above', from the spiritual world, and giving birth to the Logos in the human and natural world. And this is shown forth iconographically by placing her between the icon of the descent of the Spirit at the Pentecost and the altar on which the presence of the incarnate God is made manifest in each eucharistic celebration. And, to complete the whole movement, what is participated in this mystery is no less than the Lord of all, the Divine Logos, the Alpha that begins and the Omega that completes the whole cycle and whose image radiates from the central medallion of the dome.

This, briefly, is the fully developed iconographic scheme of the church, where the whole liturgical nature of the art of the icon is most evident. But the same principles, applied here on a fully developed scale, are also those which determine even single icons used for personal devotions: they are all means for conveying and indeed for actually bringing about in the beholder a realization and experience of the truths of the Christian faith. And it will at once be clear from what has been said that in doing this—in depicting this marriage of the Divine and the human, of eternity and time—the icon has to conform to very precise rules. Not only is the disposition of the icons in the whole iconographic scheme of the church determined by their liturgical function in the way we have noted, but the formal rules according to which each single icon has to be painted are equally strict.

Indeed, as was said at the beginning of this chapter, it is the quality of its form which makes an icon an icon, and not simply a religious picture. Moreover, for an icon to be an icon, we said, its form must derive from spiritual vision, from spiritual understanding. We like to think that because the Spirit is free to blow where He will He can therefore be expressed in any form; and we interpret this as giving a liberty to the artist to choose what form he likes for his work. The icon is based on a very different understanding of things. It is based on the idea that a spiritual vision expresses itself necessarily in a certain formal language, and that deviation from this language distorts or obscures the vision. Far from the individual artist choosing the form, it is the spiritual reality that is to be expressed which itself chooses, or imposes, the form in which the artist must express it.

This principle is made clear, both in a literal and in a symbolic fashion, in the existence of those icons which are known as 'made without hands', 'αχειροποίητες. The best Mandilion. The king of Edessa, Abgar, it will be remembered, being unable to see Christ in person, had asked for his portrait, and this Christ had sent him miraculously impressed on a piece of material. And there are several other icons also called *acheiropiiti* because the holy persons they represent have themselves impressed their images on to the material from which the icon has been made. But the miracle which occurs in these cases in an absolute sense also occurs in a relative sense in the case of every icon that is painted: it is the prototype of the icon which impresses its own image on the material.

This is only another way of saying that spiritual realities have a certain definite formal equivalent, certain fixed canons of proportion which have to be obeyed by the iconographer. Whereas in non-iconographic art the picture is generally conceived as expressing the artist's own response to or observation of his subject, it is more true in the case of an icon to think of the sacred subject itself projecting or reflecting itself on to the material of the icon. The form in which this is done then becomes the established form for that particular subject, and is 'canonized' as such by tradition. It must be remembered in this connection that the material onto which the sacred subject projects or reflects itself should be thought of as including the individual personality of the artist as well as the whole cultural and psychic ambience in which he lives. It is the difference in material in this sense that accounts for the variations between icons expressing the same subject.

Yet these variations—although in retrospect they allow us to study stylistic sequences, date various works, discuss influences, and so on—are incidental. What is important is what is intrinsic and constant in spite of these variations, and this is the formal element, which where the iconographic tradition is living will tend to reduce to a minimum all variations due to the individual personality and the cultural environment of the artist. That is why to those who are used, as we are used, to the countless modes and mannerisms of modern art, as well as to the idea that an artist is free to express what he likes how he likes, the formal control determining the icon appears an unnatural imposition. What we forget when we think like this is that the rules and canons to which the iconographer must conform are not his own or anyone else's invention, but exist in the nature of things; that there is a science of forms as precise as mathematics or astrology; and that as the iconographer's concern is to convey not his own opinions or reactions but the intrinsic nature of things, he can fulfil his task only on condition that he employs the forms in which that nature has chosen to express itself.

This does not mean that the iconographer merely imitates or copies in a servile and academic manner certain prescribed images. Such a process would result inevitably in a lifeless or decadent kind of art—one in which the forms are no longer experienced and energized by the artist. If what is to be expressed remains always one and the same, and if the iconographic forms are themselves determined, none the less a condition of whether an icon is living or dead is whether the artist himself is spiritually prepared for his task; is how far the artist himself is able to paint in and from the spirit. For the likeness of the holy figure or theme which the artist has to copy is a spiritual likeness and exists only in the spirit; and a knowledge of it is not to be obtained by empirical observation or reaction, but only through an inward merging or identification with it. The artist, that is, has to become one with that which he is to represent.

In other words there is here no distinction between art and contemplation. The artist must raise his vision from earthly to divine concerns and perceptions until he can mentally entertain the form which he is to imitate—until this form lives within him with its own inherent vitality. There has to be an endless renewal and repetition of the internal imaginative act, an endless recreation within the life of the artist of the spiritual realities which are the subject of his work and which must spontaneously inform his work if it is to live. The iconographic form—the ascertained rules of the art—are simply the means spontaneously assumed by these realities in order to express themselves.

Naturally, this expression is, as we said, modified by the personality and environment of the artist. But this intrusion of the artist's local conditions is something quite different from the wilful and arbitrary self-expression often indulged in by modern artists. The iconographer does not lay claim to that independence of and superiority to discipline which is so much a part of the modern deification of 'artistic genius'. He is concerned not with expressing himself in any superficial sense, but with revealing those forms which issue, spontaneously and universally, from his own experience of the basic truths of the Christian faith; and his one thought is, or should be, to be moved only by these forms, for what they express is that ultimate freedom and spontaneity which lie at the heart of his own being as of all other beings.

Thus we return to the point which this chapter has sought repeatedly to stress, that is to the icon as a means both for presenting a spiritual doctrine and for bringing about a spiritual realization. For in the first place the icon depicts what we have called the Christian world-picture. It illustrates the Christian creed. Like the creed it presents a theology, a doctrine of creation, and an account of the divine-human events—the 'descent from heaven', the Incarnation, the Crucifixion, the Burial, the Resurrection, and Pentecost—which together compose the Christian scheme of salvation. In this respect the icon instructs in the dogmatic truths of the Christian faith. It helps to make us conscious of the whole intellectual framework—the whole framework of ideas and beliefs—within which the Christian mystery unfolds. Unless we first have some understanding of what these are, we are hardly likely to see the point or purpose of the Christian mystery. The icon reveals and reminds us of them. It is a sign pointing towards them, towards a knowledge of those beliefs and ideas with which the Christian faith is concerned.

Second, the icon, as a crucial aspect of the liturgy, assists in delivering the individual worshipper from the constraints and illusions of clock-measured time and profane history by initiating him directly into the dimension of liturgical time and sacred history. This is too big a theme to be elucidated here in depth. Suffice it to say that the ideas and beliefs that the icon represents are not static or abstract—'Platonic ideas' in the sense that these are too often, though mistakenly, regarded. Rather they must be understood as living archetypal realities, what we have called states of being or might better call centres of power within man as well as in the universe. And these states of being or centres of power, as well as the events in which they are made manifest, are all personalized—indeed, are all persons. But since it is the same archetypes that are exemplified in each liturgical celebration; since these celebrations and the events composing them are homologous with each other, and these events are personalized, it follows that all this together must mean that the time to which the liturgy introduces us is not that in which one moment succeeds another, each disappearing into a vanishing and irreversible past. On the contrary, it is a time which is that of those individual figures whose personal presence occurs and recurs in every liturgical celebration, and which thus constitutes a liturgical time that is totally other than the time measured by clocks or which composes what we call history.

This is to say that because what happens in the liturgy happens through the recurring presence of the same archetypal figures, the liturgy does not merely commemorate an event or events that happened once and for all in the past. The events—which are persons—that the liturgy evokes do not occur in the past: they occur in the present which is their time and is a time which they themselves determine. This is why the liturgy does not merely commemorate an event. It *is* that event, and the event is the person or persons that enacts or enact the same archetypal ritual in a time that is essentially their time. And this is shown forth in the icon, which is simultaneously both the revelation of the archetype of the event—the person—it depicts, and the depiction of the event—or person—as archetype.

Finally, as the image of the personalized centres of power that constitute the event it exemplifies, the icon is penetrated with something of the vitality of its prototype. It becomes in its turn a centre of power, an incarnation in its own right of the spiritual energy of this prototype. Because this is so—because the icon vehicles in this way an energy that is more than human—it is able to induce in the worshipper a consciousness of this more than human life which it embodies. Expressing through the beauty of its line and colour the purpose of man, it also helps man to a realization of that purpose, to an understanding and experience of something of the reality of which it is the expression. Its holy personages come forth ready to bless and liberate—ready to convert the beholder from his restricted and limited point of view to the full view of their spiritual vision. For the art of the icon is ultimately so to transform the person who moves towards it that he no longer opposes the worlds of eternity and time, of spirit and matter, of the Divine and the human, but sees them as united in one Reality, in that ageless image-bearing light in which all things live, move and have their being.

7

THE ART OF TRANSFIGURATION

✠

A word that occurs and recurs in the chapters of this book, and is indeed intimately allied to the very idea of the sacred, is the word transfiguration. Patently, transfiguration, or the action it denotes, is crucial to the whole pattern of thought which underlies the themes explored in this book. It is also a word that is beginning to come into fashion. At the same time, it is a word whose meaning is probably far from clear in the minds of many people who use it. This is all the more the case because although the action it denotes is central to the destiny of man and of the whole created world as this is envisaged in the Christian tradition, its significance—for reasons which I attempt to indicate in a later part of this chapter—has been greatly obscured by the theological concepts that by and large have dominated Christian thought in its western form, whether Roman Catholic or Protestant. Hence the need to give some account of what is meant by transfiguration according to those who have meditated on it most profoundly.

I said that the idea of transfiguration is central to the Christian understanding of man's destiny as well as of the destiny of the whole created world—the one involves the other; and that this is so is confirmed by the fact that the Christian Saviour exemplifies it in His own life as recorded in the account of His transfiguration on Mount Tabor, in the New Testament. 'And after six days Jesus took with Him Peter and James and John his brother, and led them up to a high mountain apart. And He was transfigured before them, and His face shone like the sun and His garments became white as light.' So reads one of the two gospel passages in which the event is recorded.[1]

Of course, like so much else that Christ exemplifies in His life, this can be, and often is, regarded as something that refers to Christ alone, and has no particular and personal significance for every human being as such. Yet if one understands that what is exemplified in the life of Christ, as recorded in the New Testament, provides the standard according to which each individual human being can assess the possibilities, intrinsic to his nature, on whose realization in his own life depends the fulfilment of his own personal destiny, then, far from being something extrinsic to him, transfiguration must signify the most intimate and exalted experience of which he is capable. For it means no less than that his whole physical being can be so irradiated with divine light that it can shine like the sun. Not only this, but since Christ exemplifies the norm for human life, it also means that there is something radically wrong with us when our whole physical being is not so irradiated.

What is being said here is that in the Transfiguration as described in the Gospels Christ does not become something which previously He had not been; He simply shows forth what He always is. And what He shows forth is what man is in his pre-fallen, or natural and normal state. No transfiguration takes place in Christ for the simple reason that Christ has never 'fallen': He is what man is prior to his assent to sin and the deformation which ensues on that. Consequently His flesh, never having been deformed or disfigured, always irradiates the glory of His invisible divinity.

This is stated clearly by one of the doctrinal masters of the Christian tradition: 'The body of Christ,' he writes, 'has never not participated in the divine glory but . . . is fully enriched with the glory of the invisible divinity, so that the glory of the Logos and the flesh are one and the same. But this which is invisibly present in the visible body is invisible to those who are still captive to their worldly selves. When therefore Christ transfigures Himself [on Mount Tabor] He does not assume that which He was not but simply manifests that which He is . . .'[2]

From this two things emerge. The first is that man's flesh—the flesh of every living man and woman—does not irradiate, as that of Christ does, divine glory because the human race, in the person of Adam, has given assent to sin and has thus deformed itself. Man—individual man or woman—no longer lives according to the norms of human life as exemplified in the person of Christ. And the second—connected with the first—is that transfiguration is something that applies, not to man in his primordial or natural state, but to man in his fallen state. The real Transfiguration described in the Gospel is that of the disciples themselves: their eyes are opened so that they are able to see the glory of God shining through Christ's human body.

These two conclusions together mean that the significance of transfiguration can be gauged only when it is set against the background of what in Christian terms is described as the fall of man or the loss of his paradisal state, which is his natural and normal state. This in its turn means that if we are to grasp the significance of transfiguration, we must first grasp what is implied in man's lapse from his normal and natural state into a state in which he is deformed and abnormal—a lapse projected and mirrored in the biblical account of the fall from Paradise, in which pre-fallen Adam represents man in his natural and normal state, and fallen Adam represents man disfigured and denaturalized.

According to our interpreters, primordial man—Adam: man in his natural state—enjoys a perfect vision of the divine realm. He is lifted in contemplation, that is to say, above the mere perception of sensory objects and the images that these objects engender in his imagination, and no obstacle impedes the radiation of divine light and energy into his being. He is interpenetrated by the divine in all his faculties, psychic and physical, pervious to its glory and wisdom, in intimate communion with God. He is, in other words, a divinized or deified being, contemplating without interruption the image of the divine in himself as in every created thing.

His fall represents the loss of this state of communion and deification. It represents the loss of his capacity to perceive the image and glory of God in himself and in every other created reality. He has in some sense closed himself to the irradiation of divine light, and his vision is obscured, darkened, capable now of perceiving only the external appearance of things, not their inward essences. His attention is consequently drawn outside himself, into endless preoccupation with sensory or material things. Even beauty, in which in his natural state he sees the manifestation of God, he now severs from its source and regards as an end in itself—in other words, as a matter of idolatry. Fallen humanity—that condition into which we are born—is a humanity that has betrayed its contemplative experience of the divine. That is why the disciples, for instance, cannot see the divine glory that irradiates the body of Christ except in a moment of special grace when the scales are lifted from their eyes and they recover their natural vision.

Again, two things emerge from this. The first is that, in the Christian perspective, human perfection is achieved through contemplation, and that to contemplate is to see God in an immediate vision. And the second is that though this contemplative experience of God has been broken by the fall, it is by no means something whose recovery is beyond the scope of man's present possibilities: as pointed out above, the events recorded in the New Testament provide the standard according to which each individual human being can assess the possibilities, intrinsic to him, on whose realization in his own life his fulfilment depends; and one of these events is the restoration to fallen man, in the persons of the disciples, of his capacity to have a direct and immediate vision of God's glory. In other words, vision of God is by no means limited to the purely eschatological manifestation of God—God's manifestation of Himself in the last days; on the contrary, it is a possibility everyone can realize in his or her own mortal life-span. He or she can still attain perfection, here and now.

It is in considering how this perfection may be attained—or re-attained—that we have to introduce another major theme of the Christian tradition, one that complements and is inextricably intertwined with the theme of transfiguration: indeed, they are two sides of the same coin. I refer to the theme of incarnation. Like other aspects of Christian doctrine—even that of transfiguration itself—incarnation is only too often regarded as something that happened uniquely in the case of Christ, and this, too, on a unique historical occasion. It is too often forgotten that to assign, or consign, any event—even the most momentous event that can be imagined—exclusively to a time in the irrevocable past is equivalent to signing its death-warrant where its dynamic influence on living men and women is concerned; and if so many of the major doctrinal themes of the Christian tradition appear today to have so little relevance, this is above all due to the fact that Christians themselves have been only too prone to regard what has been paradigmatically exemplified in the life of Christ, and is intended to be valid for all human beings, as something that relates to Christ alone and not—except indirectly—to man as such, quite apart from the particular historical period in which he happens to live.

The Incarnation is a case in point, perhaps the most glaring case in point. It is not a question of denying that in the historical figure of Christ God took on a human form. But what is important is to disengage from its historical exemplification in the person of Christ the significance that this particular event has with respect to the perennial or eternal—trans-historical—relationship between God and man, the Divine and the human, and what it reveals about their dynamic reciprocity and interpenetration. What is in question, in other words, is again the possibility inherent in human nature that is revealed through the Incarnation.

From this point of view, then, what the Incarnation—or the idea of incarnation—affirms is the possibility for men and women to reverse the process set in motion by the fall. If the fall denotes a lapse in the relationship between God and man, the Divine and the human, in the sense that the divinizing energies of God, intrinsic to man as created in the image of God, are no longer active or operative within man in such a way that they illumine his whole being, soul and body, and permit him a direct and immediate vision of the divine glory which is also his own glory, then the Incarnation signifies the healing of this breach. It signifies the process whereby man's attention—his whole being—is drawn back to the contemplation of the realities obscured for him by the fall. From this angle what the Incarnation presents, or represents, is the gradual unfolding of the divine within the human, even within the physical human body; and the stages—the initiatory stages, they might be called—through which this unfolding is accomplished are shown forth in the Gospels.

This is the movement which is typified in the life of Christ, and is synoptically described by, for instance, St Athanasios in his treatise on the Incarnation: 'Once the intelligence had diverted its attention towards sensory things, the Logos humbled Himself in order to appear in a body, so that as man He could draw men towards Him, and incline their minds towards Him, and persuade them by His acts—for they saw Him as a man—that He was not simply man but also God, the Logos and Wisdom of the true God.'[3] Once one grasps that incarnation involves as it were a downward movement on the part of God—a movement through which God veils His glory by clothing Himself in the 'flesh' because only thus is man able to participate in that process through which his attention is raised from the sensory to the intelligible, from the visible to the invisible, from the created to the uncreated, by means of the drama unfolded in the life of Christ as portrayed in the Gospels—then one can also grasp why the theme of incarnation is so intimately intertwined with that of transfiguration. For what transfiguration presupposes is a corresponding upward movement on the part of man, a movement through which he gradually sheds the veils of his own ignorance and blindness in order to disclose the image of God within himself and to clothe himself in God's glory. In other words, incarnation and transfiguration determine each other reciprocally. Without incarnation there would be no transfiguration—no recovery of the vision of God; but equally without transfiguration there would be no incarnation—no revitalizing by God of the divine energies within man's soul and body so that his whole being radiates with the Divinity made incarnate.

From this last statement it should be possible to see how these two complementary and reciprocal themes of incarnation and transfiguration are themselves subsumed in the third major doctrinal theme of the Christian tradition, the theme of deification—theosis—or resurrection; for the theme of deification or resurrection concerns precisely the process according to which man attains a mystical perception of God and through this perception comes himself to participate, soul and body, in the divine glory. The stages through which this process is consummated are described by the masters of Christian spirituality as those of purification, contemplation, and illumination, or union. A detailed study of what is accomplished in each of these stages, and the way it is accomplished, lies beyond the scope of our present purpose, though something of what they involve will be indicated below. What should be noted, however, is that the goal of both transfiguraton and deification—vision of and conscious participation in the Divine—themselves presuppose the recognition of two other doctrinal principles.

The first may be introduced as follows. A cardinal feature of Christian doctrine is its insistence on the ultimate unknowability and inaccessability of the Divine—of God's essential nature or His essence. One authority affirms this with particular eloquence: 'For as intelligible things are incomprehensible and invisible to sensory things, and simple formless things to those that have figure and form . . . so in the same way the supra-essential indetermination [the divine essence] is beyond all beings and the unity above intelligence is beyond all intelligences, the goodness beyond words cannot be expressed in any words . . .. A unity unifying all unity, a supra-essential essence, an unintelligible intelligence and a meaningless meaning—unreason and unintelligence and unnameability, not being according to any being, and yet being the cause of the being of all things—it itself is not, seeing that it surpasses all that is . . .. Accordingly one must not dare to say or think anything about the supra-essential and hidden Divinity except what has been divinely revealed to us . . .. '[4] Another interpreter, in a passage on transfiguration, says the same thing more succinctly: 'Thus the light on the face of our Lord . . . is the symbol of the apophatic mystical theology according to which God in His essence transcends all thought and is more than unknowable and is infinitely beyond all infinity . . .. For it is not in the nature of what is uncreated to be contained by what is created, nor of what is infinite to be conceived in all respects by finite beings.'[5]

If one reads these passages and the many others in a similar strain that occur in the works of the great Christian exegetists, one might conclude that they were agnostics of one kind or another. Certainly, at all events, what they say seems to be at odds with the reality they affirm in their three major doctrinal themes—incarnation, transfiguration and deification: for if by definition there is nothing divine and uncreated that the human can know and in which it can participate—if God is unknowable and inaccessible—there then can be no incarnation, transfiguration or deification as these same exegetists understand the terms, for all three of them involve both direct knowledge of and direct participation in the Divine, in the fullest sense of the words.

Unless, therefore, these exegetists are to be accused of self-contradiction—in fact, unless Christian doctrine as such is to be accused of self-contradiction—there must be a way in which their teaching on the unknowability and inaccessibility of the Divine can be reconciled with their teaching on the three major doctrinal themes here being considered. Indeed, however fond they may be of paradox and however much their thought may at times ignore the formal rules of logic, they are not likely to be so stupid as to assert on the one hand a proposition that on the other hand makes it impossible for their central anthropological and soteriological themes to have any basis in reality.

What this means is that if these themes are to have a basis in reality, then it cannot be impossible for the human being to know and participate in what is divine and uncreated. Or to put this the other way round: there must be in God that which the human can know and that in which it can participate. This in its turn means that God cannot be defined simply in terms of His essence, for this by definition *is* unknowable, inaccessible, and beyond all participation.

That in fact there is no self-contradiction in the teaching of these doctrinal masters on the themes in question is because they evince in the Divine a distinction which they regard as axiomatic. This is the distinction between the divine essence on the one hand and the divine energy, or operation or activity, on the other—the energy or operation or activity by and through which God creates, nourishes and sustains His creation. This distinction is an integral part of their theology. In fact it is an integral part of what for them constitutes the very nature of things, for they take it for granted that there cannot be an essence without its corresponding energy—that it is precisely the energy that actualizes and concretizes the essence of a being, and that without the energy the essence can have no reality, no subsistance. 'All energy,' writes one of these masters, 'is defined as the essential activity of a substance . . . [and] who has ever heard of a substance that is without activity and totally inert, or who has encountered an energy that is not the activity of a subsistent power?'[6]

It is in accordance with this understanding that another master writes, 'We speak of knowing God through His energies, not of knowing Him according to His essence. For His energies descend down to us, but His essence is inaccessible.'[7] And St John Chrysostomos, speaking of St John the Evangelist, writes, 'This is why he [John] does not name God's essence anywhere, for it is not possible to say what the essence of God is. Throughout he shows God to us according to His energies.'[8]

At this point a certain discretion is required. If the authorities to whom I refer make this distinction between essence and energy; if they say that while the former is inaccessible the latter descends down to us, or that while the essence is unknowable and cannot be given a name, the energy is knowable and has a name, or that while the essence cannot be participated in, the energy can be, they do not on that account posit any form of dualism or dichotomy between essence and energy. For them the divine energy is just as inexhaustible and infinite as the essence. Nor do they posit some kind of composition in God, or imply in any way that there is a radical difference between essence and energy—that, for instance, the essence is uncreated, while the energy is created, or that the essence represents a superior mode of the Divinity, while the energy represents an inferior mode. All that is affirmed is that it is by means of His energy that we know and participate in God, and that it is to the extent that this energy penetrates into us that we penetrate into the Divine.

As is evident from some of the citations given, another characteristic of the divine energy is that, unlike the divine essence, it is multiple. One can speak of the divine energies. This is confirmed in the writings attributed to St Dionysios the Areopagite, where it is said that the Divinity 'never abandons its own unique intimacy, but in order to commix . . . with those over whom it watches it multiplies itself and goes out of itself, while yet remaining at the interior of itself solidly and stably established in motionless self-identity'.[9] St Basil the Great says simply, 'The energies are diverse, the essence is simple'; and he protests both against those who would compound the energies and against those who confuse the energies with the essence: 'Is the terror that God inspires the same as His love for men? Or are His justice, and His creative power, and His foreknowledge, and His retribution, and His magnificence and His providence all the same? And when we speak of one of these things, are we speaking of the essence?'[10]

All this may seem remote from the theme of transfiguration. Yet it is necessary to speak of it, because otherwise it might be difficult to see in what way transfiguration can be a vision of God—a vision that involves a knowledge of and participation in God—without this appearing to disrupt God's essential unity and simplicity. Unless the distinction between the entirely simple non-participable essence and the multiple, participable energies is acknowledged, how can every created being, as created being, share in the Divine without splintering the unity of the Divine into a myriad fragments? If the distinction in question is born in mind, it can be understood that God is not one in an arithmetical sense, and He is simple not in the sense that nothing can be distinguished in His Divinity. He is one and simple because He is indivisible, essence and energies constituting an indissoluble, seamless and indivisible whole.

The second doctrinal principle which the reality of both transfiguration and deification presupposes is a distinction, from the human side, in types of knowledge. Direct vision of and participation in the Divine involve, as has already been affirmed on several occasions, a knowledge of God. But one has to specify what kind of knowledge is meant; and in this respect our authorities distinguish between two kinds of knowledge, the one very different from the other. The Areopagitic writings make this distinction very clearly: 'One must realize that our intelligence has a capacity for thought according to which it knows intelligible things; but there is also a union which transcends the [natural] capacity of our intelligence and by means of which our intelligence is unified to things that surpass it.'[11]

The first of these types of knowledge is what one might call a theoretical knowledge, that of conceptualization. But vision of God—or knowledge of God—which is intrinsic to transfiguration, is not this kind of knowledge. It is a supra-rational knowledge, one that requires a transcendence of all conceptualized knowledge—one indeed that requires a certain going out of, or going beyond, the limits of one's created nature, into a unity that is a kind of ignorance. It should be added that we are here presupposing an anthropology which accepts the Pauline tripartite idea of man as spirit, soul and body, in which the spirit is regarded as a supra-rational faculty. That is why it is possible to speak of man attaining a knowledge of realities which strictly speaking are neither sensory nor intelligible, neither physical nor psychic, and which belong in fact to the realm of the divine uncreated energies.

Yet it is precisely because these realities do pertain to this realm and transcend the intelligence as well as the senses, the soul as well as the body, that—paradox as it may appear—they can be perceived and known by the whole man, body and soul and something in him which is more than either. There is a materialization of the Divine which is simultaneously a spiritualization of the material—of all that is created, body and soul. Man is raised towards God in a movement which is simultaneously a descent of God towards man—in that coincidence of transfiguration and incarnation in which his deification is consummated. 'God is light, and He communicates His radiance to those who are united with Him, to the extent to which they are purified. Then the extinguished light of the soul (that is to say, the darkened spirit or image of God in man) knows that it is rekindled, because the divine fire has embraced it . . .. Man is united to God spiritually and corporeally, for his soul is in no way separated from the spirit, nor the body from the soul. God enters into union with the whole man.'[12] 'And we shall become as gods, joined in intimacy to God, showing no stain on our body but all being in likeness to the whole body of Christ, each one of us having as our limbs the complete Christ. For the One is made many, and the One yet remains undivided, but each part is indeed the whole Christ.'[13]

The last two quotations are from the writings of St Simeon the New Theologian (949–1022), a mystic privileged not only to live through the experience of transfiguration but also to express its meaning in prose and poetry; and at this point therefore it may be appropriate briefly to supplement what has so far been presented in somewhat theoretical terms with a more experiential and existential account of the same mystery, recapitulated in St Simeon's own words. St Simeon unites the mythic perspective within which transfiguration should be envisaged with the expression in personal terms of his experiences of some of the major phases of the initiatory drama in which he is involved.

As explained above, the significance of transfiguration can be truly assessed only when it is set against the background—or within the perspective—of what in Christian terms is described as the fall of man or the loss of his paradisal state, which is his natural and normal state. It is consequently with what he understands by this fall and its implications that St Simeon begins. 'In the beginning' God made the earth—the whole earth, St Simeon explains, not just Eden, not just Paradise. The scriptures, he writes, 'do not say that God made Paradise, nor that He said, Let it be born, but they say that He planted Paradise. And He made spring from the ground every tree beautiful to look at, and delicious to taste, having various fruits which never decayed and never gave out, but were always freshly tender, and very sweet and gave to the first-created beings great pleasure and nourishment, because it was fit to give uncorruptible food to bodies of the first-made beings which were themselves incorruptible. Thus was their life without tiredness and without labour in Paradise.'[14]

Yet the first man—archetypal man, Adam—was not just a passive creature, created to do nothing but enjoy a pre-ordained and irresponsible idleness. On the contrary, he was a created god, an organ whose purpose it was to absorb still further the flesh into the spirit, to bring all to still greater perfection. But by an act of false judgment—by setting up his own will, his own ego, in opposition to the power that created him—he forfeited his original splendour, and was driven from Eden. And through his own transgression he brought also into the earth—not into Paradise, which remains always as it was—dislocation and revolt. This is how St Simeon describes that event: 'Thus all creation, when it saw that Adam was driven from Paradise, did not wish to serve him any longer; the sun did not want to shine on him, nor the moon, nor did the stars want to come out, nor springs to pour forth water, nor rivers to run. The wind sought not to blow any longer, so that sinful Adam should not breathe. The beasts and all creatures on earth, when they saw Adam stripped of his first glory, despised him, and everything at once shook over his head; the heavens were ready to fall upon him and earth desired to support him no longer.'[15]

Man now is condemned to live in this 'fallen' world which he himself has created. He no longer enjoys the happiness that was once his. And for St Simeon, one of the saddest marks of the fall is man's loss of independence. He is no longer his own master, but a mere victim of needs to which he must submit or die, and which drive him hither and thither in desperate anxiety. 'Because man,' he writes, 'on account of his transgression of God's commandment, became corruptible, and mortal, and naturally hungers, and thirsts, and grows tired, and labours, and gets cold, and gets hot—for this, without wishing it, he eats, and drinks, and sleeps, and rests, and dresses, and undresses, whether he wants to or not. And no man is able to endure hunger, or thirst, or even the smallest of those things of which we spoke, except by force and with great distress.'[16]

Again, for St Simeon another of the terrible things about this fallen state is the fact that everything in life perishes and decays, everything which man loves and trusts and relies on for his happiness. 'All things of the world', he writes, 'perish and pass away like dreams, and there is nothing stable or sure. The sun, and the stars, and the sky, and the earth, and everything goes by, and from them all only man is left. What then of all those things can be of use to us at the hour of death's need, when we go from this present life to eternal rest, and leave all these things here, and they decay, and vanish? And if it happens that visible things do not vanish, what is their use to us, since we depart from them and leave here only our dead and senseless body, and our soul is not able to see any longer through our body, or to be seen by anything else at all.'[17] And he writes in a poem of this anxiety of a man who separates himself from the source of life:

A strange and most astonishing thing have I heard:
non-physical nature more hard than stone
suffered a change, as if a diamond
unsoftened by fire or iron
should become wax mixed with lead.
Lately I believed a small trickle of water
took years to hollow the rock's strength,
but really nothing in life is changeless.
From now on let no one think to cheat me.
Alas to him who sees the fleeting things of life
as permanent, and is content with them.
He, as my wretched self, will be misled.
Night from my most sweet brother has estranged me,
cutting love's uncut light.[18]

To recover the light—that is the task for man. And it is

because of this that, as we have seen, the themes of incarnation, transfiguration and deification—or resurrection—are so crucial. As we have also noted, these events are not only, or even mainly, events which have happened once, in the past. They are entirely present and should be experienced by everyone. Christ's life represents in figure, as an archetype in the Platonic sense, what man actually is; it is the incarnate symbol of each man's proper destiny. Christ, or life, or light—the terms are interchangeable—was joined to the world, St Simeon writes, 'as yeast, as a small offering in the dough of our nature, and He joined our nature with His own incomprehensible, unapproachable nature, and, to explain things better, He joined all the reality of His divinity substantially to our nature, and that human nature He mixed unmixably with His own substance, and He made it a holy temple to Himself.'[19]

In another sermon, on the occasion of Easter, St Simeon goes on to speak of Christ being buried in us as 'in the tomb', and of how in image He gave the pattern for man's inmost life: 'Christ and our God, after He was hanged upon the Cross, and had nailed to it the world's sin, and had died, went down to the bottom parts of Hades. When then He came up from Hades, He went back into his immaculate body (from which even when He went down to Hades He was not separated), and at once He rose from the dead, and then ascended into Heaven with great glory and power. And so now, when we go out from this world and, assimilating to ourselves the suffering of the Lord, enter into the tomb of repentance, and of humility, then the same Christ comes down from the heavens, and enters into our body, as into a tomb, and joins Himself to our souls, and raises them up from there where they were obviously dead, and so gives joy to him who resurrects himself in this way with Christ, seeing the glory of his secret resurrection. Thus then the resurrection of Christ is our resurrection who were fallen into sin and dead. For how is it possible for Christ to be resurrected, since He did not fall into sin, nor change Himself completely?'[20] And elsewhere St Simeon declares that crucifixion and death 'are nothing else than the perfect mortification and cutting off of our own self-will',[21] and that resurrection of our soul is 'union with life'.[22]

How man achieves that union is for St Simeon something quite straightforward. It does not, he repeats many times, demand great learning or erudition. The Spirit of God is revealed, he writes, 'not to the rhetoricians or philosophers, not to those learned in the writings of the Greeks, not to those studying foreign works, but to the poor in spirit and in life, to the pure in heart and in body.'[23] And he quotes the words of an elder saint: 'Know, my child, that God does not rejoice very much either in fasts, or in watches, or in other bodily labours, or in any other good work, nor does He reveal Himself to anything other than to a humble and an unmeddling disposition, and to a good soul and heart.'[24]

Yet this humility which for St Simeon is the cornerstone of man's spiritual development is not a feeling of worthlessness or of man's nothingness. It is something rather which results from man's sense of the abyss which separates his desire for fulfilment from fulfilment itself, something also which results from his dizzying awareness of his own potentialities. And if humility is the cornerstone, the base of spiritual progress, the roof, the crown, to be reached by the steps of silence and prayer, is love. 'O all-desired love,' St Simeon writes, 'blessed is he who loves you because he will never desire to love much any human beauty. Blessed is he who entwines himself with you out of divine passion, so that he gives up all the world, and approaching everyone is not defiled. Blessed is he who kisses your beauties and with great longing enjoys them, for he wishes to make holy his soul with undefiled blood and with the waters that fall from you. Blessed is he who caresses you with longing, because he wishes to change himself spiritually . . . for you are the unspeakable joy. Blessed is he who obtains you, for he will not opt for the treasures of this world, because you are truly inexhaustible wealth.'[25]

This love is also an illumination, an ecstasy. Here we touch the heart of the mystical experience and that which even the mystics themselves find hard to put into words. Perhaps the best way to describe it is as a relationship between one person and another person heightened to an intensity beyond that which is possible on the merely mortal level. That at least is how many mystics have described it. There is, for instance, the song of Solomon from the Old Testament, the Song of Songs: 'My beloved is mine and I am his: he feedeth among the lilies. Until the day break, and the shadows flee away, turn, my beloved, and be thou like a roe or a young hart upon the mountains of Bether.' Or there is the soul's song to the bridegroom of St John of the Cross:

> I have prepared my soul for him,
> my abundance is in his service;
> I do not keep flocks,
> nor have other work,
> for now my exercise is love alone.

St Simeon's own language to express this relationship does not have perhaps the same richness of poetic imagery. His relationship is with the light, the 'phos'. It is a more impassible relationship. To the affective mysticism of Eros, he unites the speculative mysticism of gnosis: 'And behold great light flashed spiritually within me, and took with it all my mind, and my soul, and I marvelled at it, the sudden miracle, and became ecstatic, and I forgot both the place where I stood, and what I was, and how, and I cried only 'Kyrie eleison', as I understood when I came to myself. But who it was who spoke, or moved my tongue, I do not know, God knows, for how I was joined to that light, with body, or without body, I do not know. That light knows, which drove from my soul all darkness, and all earthly care, and freed me from all coarse matter and from the weight of the body, which had made my limbs languid and very slack. For so much it tautened, that terrible wonder, and strengthened the slackness which because of much labour my limbs and nerves then had, that it seemed to me that I had put off a dress of corruption . . .. And that light when it appears, rejoices, and when it hides itself, it wounds, and gives much pain. And it comes close to me, and raises me to the heavens. A pearl it is, and clothes me with light. And it seems within me like a star, and is undivided in all creation;

it flashes like the sun, and I understand how all creation is held together through its power; it shows me everything that is in creation and it orders me not to go beyond the limits of human nature . . .. '[26] And, he says in another place, when that power comes into you, 'then the soul sees, as in a mirror, even its smallest faults, and knows great humility, and thinking of the boundless glory of God, fills with all joy and gladness, and is amazed at that unhoped for miracle, and sheds springs of tears. And thus all the man is changed, and knows God, and is known first by God, for only the grace of the Holy Spirit makes man scorn all earthly things and things of the sky, and the present, and future, and sorrows and joys, and makes him a friend of God, and son of the Highest, and god by grace.'[27]

St Simeon speaks of this transfiguration in one of his poems:

> But now things more terrible attend:
> limbs of Christ we are and Christ is our own limbs,
> and Christ is my poor hand and Christ is my poor foot,
> and I myself a hand and foot of Christ:
> I move my hand and Christ is all my hand,
> undivided seems divinity in me:
> I move my foot and, see, it flashes like Him.
> Say not I blaspheme, but reveal these things,
> and worship Christ, yourself achieving this:
> for if you wish you will become His limbs,
> and thus the limbs of every one of us
> become the limbs of Christ and Christ our very limbs;
> and every ugly thing is filled with grace,
> clothed with heavenly loveliness and splendour,
> and we become as gods with God united.[28]

And in another short poem, he describes a man thus perfected:

> Solitary, one who is unmixed with the world,
> and continually speaks with God alone.
> Seeing he is seen, loving he is loved,
> and becomes light glittering unspeakably.

Praised, he feels himself more poor,
and being close, yet goes a stranger.
O miracle strange in every way and inexplicable.
For immense richness, I exist penniless,
and having as I think nothing, possess much,
and I say I thirst, in the midst of waters.[29]

This is the summit of the deific experience, the transfiguration through which man is reborn at the springhead of his own being.

This, then, is something of the art of transfiguration. But one further question remains to be asked: if the theme of transfiguration as presented in this study is so close to the heart of Christian spirituality, that it may be said to constitute its essence, why does it receive such relatively scant attention in western Christian speculation—so scant indeed that its import and significance are virtually erased in the western Christian consciousness?

Although this question is not one that can be answered fully here, I think it can be said that the main reason why the theme of transfiguration has been so ignored is that its implications, doctrinal and other, tend to cut across what has become part and parcel of western Christian theory and practice. First, under what might be called Erasmian influences this theory and practice have been somewhat domesticated, in that it is felt that the Christian life can be adequately lived without any need to transcend our 'natural' and animal functions or the dimensions of the ordinary space-time world. This correspondingly means that it is felt that the Christian life can be best fulfilled in terms of good works and pastoral service, especially in some collective or social form. The idea that a precondition of fulfilling the Christian life is a radical rebirth or regeneration of the kind signified by transfiguration has been progressively eroded. We don't take too literally the admonition:

Though Christ in Bethlehem town
A thousand times were born,
Till He be born in thee
Thy life is but forlorn.

On the contrary, we prefer the stance commended by people like Isaac Watts:

> God is in heaven, and men below;
> Be short our tunes, our words be few;
> A sacred reverence checks our songs,
> And praise sits silent on our tongues.

In short, the way of contemplation is no longer commonly regarded as *par excellence* the way to Christian perfection. It is felt that the distinction between 'divine' and 'human' is virtually an absolute one, and cannot be diminished or modified, and that a statement like 'we remain creatures while becoming God by Grace' is to push paradox into the realms of the nonsensical.

Such an attitude may be the consequence of the hold that the kind of redemption theory associated with St Anselm has had on the western Christian consciousness. For what this theory above all emphasizes is the humanity of the incarnate God. That is why the idea of Christ as the sacrificial victim plays so great a part in it. Christ, our High Priest, must have something to offer by way of atonement for man's sin, and this living sacrifice is focused in His humanity: Christ is a saving and atoning victim offering His own manhood to the Father. But for Christ to be in a position to offer His manhood in this way must mean that He possesses a manhood so distinct from His divinity that it can be conceived as a substance virtually independent of His divinity.

What is implicit in this theory is the notion that Christ is both God *and* man, as two virtually distinct and independent substances, and this dualistic Christology is far stronger than the Christology that envisages Christ as a union or synthesis of the Divine and the human or as the Theanthropos. There is no word in western Christian terminology that adequately expresses the idea of the mutual interpenetration of the divine and the human in Christ in the way that the Greek term, *perichoresis,* expresses it. This means that whether one is talking about the Divine and the human in Christ or the Divine and the material elements in the

Eucharist, the tendency is to see the elements or substances involved as juxtaposed and not as inextricably interpenetrating; and this is reflected in an anthropology in which it is possible to envisage man in a state of sin totally cut off from God, totally deprived of grace, so much so that he can be 'saved' or 'redeemed' only by a gratuitous and as it were extrinsic act of God. In other words, man's fallen state is in this perspective regarded as his natural and normal state, not as an unnatural and abnormal state from which he must escape by resuscitating the latent divinity that in his natural state is fully active or energized within him.

Such a conception of the relationship between the Divine and the human, reflected in the theory of redemption of which we have been speaking, does of course make the idea of transfiguration or deification, with all its implications, difficult if not impossible to accept. Because what this latter idea presupposes is precisely a Christology that insists on the union or interpenetration of the Divine and the human in Christ and hence on an anthropology in which man in his natural state is regarded as a being in whom the Divine and the human interact and reciprocate each other in a similar manner, to such a degree that it is impossible to envisage the human without including the Divine or the Divine without including the human.

In other words, the idea of the theanthropic union in Christ—that he is the Theanthropos, rather than a being who is both God *and* man—is reflected in an anthropology that assumes a certain natural affinity between God and man even after the fall. Fallen humanity may have lost its original status of filial deification, but it has not lost the possibility of becoming re-established in divine sonship and it has not lost either the natural, intrinsic grace of free will through which it can respond to the call to re-establish this sonship. This means that in this perspective it is impossible to divide the divine from the human to the extent of envisaging that man through sin is, or may be, totally cut off from God or totally deprived of grace. The affinity between God and man—the divine image in man—always persists: by definition there can be no man without this affinity or this image within him, however inoperative, or unenergized, it may have become. This is why in this perspective redemption not only can mean but actually, essentially and centrally does mean transfiguration, a rebirth—of which the paradigm is revealed in and by the incarnate Logos on Mount Tabor—in the life and light of the Triune God Himself.

NOTES

1. Matthew 17:1–2.
2. St John of Damaskos, 'Homily on the Transfiguration', 12–13. P. G. xcvi, 564–5.
3. St Athanasios, *On the Incarnation*, 16. P. G. xxv, 124.
4. St Dionysios the Areopagite, *The Divine Names*, 1, 1–2. P. G. iii, 588.
5. St Maximos the Confessor, P. G. xci, 1167.
6. St John of Damaskos, *On the Orthodox Faith*, 59. P. G. xciv, 1057.
7. St Basil the Great, *To Amphilochios*, Letter 234. P. G. xxxii, 869.
8. St John Chrysostomos, *Homilies on John*, 2, 4. P. G. lix, 34.
9. St Dionysios the Areopagite, *The Celestial Hierarchy*, 1, 2. P. G. iii, 121.
10. St Basil the Great, *To Amphilochios*, Letter 234. P. G. xxxii, 869.
11. St Dionysios the Areopagite, *The Divine Names*, vii. P. G. iii, 865.
12. St Simeon the New Theologian, *Ta Apanta* (Thessaloniki, 1969), I Homily 25, p. 135.
13. St Simeon the New Theologian, P. G. cxx, 532bc, cited by J. M. Hussey, *Church and Learning in the Byzantine Empire 867–1185* (1937), p. 223.
14. St Simeon the New Theologian, *Ta Apanta*, op. cit, I, Homily 45, p. 208.
15. Ibid, I, Homily 45, p. 209
16. Ibid, I, Homily 5, p. 48
17. Ibid, I, Homily 19, pp. 110–111. See also Homily 3, p. 40.
18. St Simeon the New Theologian, Hymn 10
19. St Simeon the New Theologian, *Ta Apanta*, op. cit, I, Homily 44, p. 210.
20. Ibid, I, Homily 42, pp. 193–194.
21. Ibid, I, Homily 73, p. 384.

22. Ibid, I, Homily 42, p. 194.

23. St Simeon the New Theologian, Letter to Stephen of Nikomedia, ed. I. Hausherr, *Vie de Syméon le Nouveau Théologien* (Rome, 1928), introduction, p. lxv.

24. St Simeon the New Theologian, *Ta Apanta*, op. cit, I, Homily 86, pp. 490–491.

25. Ibid, I, Homily 43, p. 272.

26. Ibid, I, Homily 86, p. 491.

27. Ibid, I, Homily 72, p. 386.

28. St Simeon the New Theologian, Hymn 15.

29. St Simeon the New Theologian, Hymn 3.

8

THE NUPTIAL MYSTAGOGY

✠

This appraisal of the nuptial relationship takes it as axiomatic that the distinction of human nature into male and female is in accordance with the wisdom and providence of God. It is not something arbitrary or accidental or that has developed in response to various pressures of a biological, environmental or other relative kind. On the contrary, it is a manifestation of an ultimate mystery hidden in the depths of divine life itself. When God created human nature He created it male and female. But the creative causes or principles of all that is created are inherent in God's own being. This is to say that the source of the distinction between man and woman lies in the fact that God embraces the principles of masculinity and femininity in Himself. He is Himself male and female. The Divine is androgynous; and, where human nature is concerned, this androgyny of the Divine is polarized in man and woman.

So fundamental indeed is this mystery of God's bisexual nature that echoes and traces of it are to be found on every level of creation, down to that of the most simple and rudimentary forms of life. But of all created beings, man is the most direct expression of the Divine. He is most fully created in the image of God. Hence it is that the principles of masculinity and femininity that co-exist in God are manifest in human nature in the most explicit way. It is as if God wished to see the mystery of His most intimate self revealed, as in a mirror, with as little distortion as possible, and the result was man and woman. It is in man and woman that God perceives the fullest expression of His own glory. His is the secret, non-articulated and formless reality of which the forms of man and woman are the disclosed and articulated images.

At this point it might be asked why, if God is bisexual,

does not this bisexuality find its most adequate expression on the human level in the creation, not of two distinct male and female beings, but of a single androgynous figure. Indeed, according to one reading it might be claimed that in the account of creation presented in the opening chapters of Genesis, which provide the starting-point for Christian speculation on this theme, such is in fact the original order of things. God creates man—and here 'man' signifies not simply the male sex but human nature in its integrity; and this human nature is bisexual: 'male and female created He them'. But it appears that these dual aspects of human nature—the 'them' in the citation—are still properties of a single being: they are embraced within the single being of Adam. Initially, at this stage of creation, there is no Eve. Or at least Eve is the feminine component of the integral and androgynous human nature which is fully manifest in the single being of Adam.

Still in accordance with Genesis, it would appear that it is only at a subsequent stage of creation that the bifurcation of the sexes takes place and the female is as it were disunited from the male and enshrined in the separate figure of Eve. And the reason given in Genesis for this bifurcation of the original androgynous Adam, and for the separating off of the feminine aspect of human nature in the independent figure of Eve, is not that such polarization of the sexes shows forth God's glory more fully. The reason given is simply the all-too-human one that Adam was alone and lacked a fitting helpmate. This would make it appear that the creation of woman as a separate being has nothing or little to do with God's desire to contemplate more fully the mystery of His most intimate self in its counterparts on the plane of creation, for He could do this most fully in the single androgynous figure of Adam. It would appear, rather, that the creation of woman as a separate being was not within the original divine intention, but was a subsequent concession on the part of God to a kind of unforseen contingency that arose after the creation of Adam. Eve's *raison d'être* lies solely in this contingency; and her function as a separate being has meaning only in so far as she relates to man as his helpmate. Apart from this, there is no real reason why she should exist.

Many Christian writers have been persuaded by this account of the creation of Adam and Eve in the Book of Genesis to regard woman as a being who is secondary and subordinate to man, who has no reason for her existence apart from man, and who would not in fact have existed had the original man—Adam—been able to preserve his own bisexual nature intact, as God had originally intended that he should. Indeed, some Christian writers have seen in the creation of Eve as a separate identity evidence of a 'fall' that took place within the original creation itself. In this view, the ideal human state is seen as represented by the androgynous Adam, who mirrors in his single being God's own androgyny and so is the divine image *par excellence*; but for reasons of economy that have to do not so much with God's own desire for self-revelation as with man's created welfare, this ideal state is in practice extrapolated in the forms of two separate human beings, Adam and Eve, who co-exist in Paradise. Woman's creation is still regarded as in accordance with the wisdom and providence of God, and woman is still a revelation or unveiling of the divine—a theophany—for the simple reason that every created thing possesses a theophanic quality. But in some sense her creation is adventitious, and she is a second best; for, ideally speaking, her creation could be subsumed and transcended in a single created being who unites and reconciles the masculine and feminine aspects of human nature in himself.

Such a conception of the ideal human state has always haunted man, not least of all within the Christian world; and many are those who have set out to attain, or regain, a mastery of what they suppose to be their original bisexual nature, lost through some catastrophe that has tragically cut this nature into two and left each half of it in an abnormal state of destitution and self-exile.[1] And it must be confessed that if God Himself is androgynous, and man is created in the image of God, then it is difficult to see how the destiny of individual man and woman is not most fully achieved when each, severally and independently, does unite and reconcile the sundered masculine and feminine aspects of human nature in a single being.

Yet to oppose this conception of the ideal human state, is it not possible to read the Genesis account of the creation of woman in another sense? The word that is used in the opening chapter of Genesis to signify that God sets the seal of His approval on the successive phases of His creation is, in the Greek translation of the Hebrew, the word *kalon*, which primarily denotes the beautiful: 'And God saw that it was beautiful'. The same Hebrew word in the authorized English versions of the text is translated as 'good': 'And God saw that it was good'. The Hebrew word itself can, it appears, mean both good and beautiful; but the Greek translation in the Septuagint emphasizes more particularly the aspect of beauty, and the Greek theological tradition has correspondingly seen in the beauty of the created world the manifestation of that divine beauty, the desire for whose expression provided as it were the motive force lying behind the original *fiat*: God's desire to reveal His formless and occulted beauty in forms in which He could delight. Hence the fittingness of what He creates—the degree to which He recognizes that it corresponds to the divine archetypes—is dependent upon its accordance with the inner harmony of His own being; for it is precisely this harmony which determines the ultimate norms of beauty. When God 'saw that it was beautiful', this seeing was an act of self-recognition by means of which He verified that what He saw was a true and faithful image of His own inner and non-manifest life.

Bearing this in mind, it is surely of great pertinence that the Genesis account of the actual creation of Eve begins with the recognition on the part of God that the presence of the single figure of Adam in Paradise was *ou kalon*, 'not beautiful', 'not good': 'And God said: the man alone is not beautiful.' Up to this point, God had seen that all was beautiful, all was good, all was in accordance with the inner harmony of His being. But at this point something was out of joint and unfitting. Creation was still a distorted or inadequate image of the divine archetype. It was still in a state of disparity and incompletion, it was still truncated, requiring a further stage of articulation if it was to reflect as fully as possible the divine archetype. And this further stage of articulation is accomplished in the creation of Eve.

If this reading of the Genesis narrative is taken into account then it can be seen that there is nothing whatsoever merely adventitious or second best in the creation of woman. Just as much as man she is the consequence of God's desire to see His glory displayed on the plane of creation as fully as possible. The bifurcation of God's androgynous nature into two distinct male and female beings is not therefore a tragedy or a fall from an ideal human state into a state that is more imperfect. On the contrary, it is the necessary and only way in which God can put as it were the finishing touch to the divine work of art in which He is engaged. Failure to put this final touch would have meant the miscarriage of the whole work; it would have meant leaving it in an arrested and incomplete state. The mastercraftsman would have failed in carrying out His intention, only to be fulfilled by bringing paradigm and artefact into as close a relationship as possible. Only subsequent to the creation of woman could God confirm that the showing forth of the plenitude and richness of human nature in the figures of Adam and Eve was in accord with the inner harmony of His nature and so was beautiful and good. It is in the mastery of his final touch that the genius of the great artist is consummated.

It would likewise follow from such a reading of the Genesis narrative that the question which provided the starting-point for this excursus—namely, whether a single androgynous figure might not more adequately reflect God's bisexuality in the human level than two distinct male and female beings—must receive a negative answer. Whatever else may apply in the case of other levels of creation—in the case of the angelic level, for instance, or of that of very elementary forms of life—it is clear that where the human level is concerned the polarization into the two figures of man and woman represents a fuller manifestation of the divine than a single androgynous figure. It is as if the two complementary principles that we describe as the masculine and the feminine principles, united and reconciled in God Himself, require this polarization on the human plane if the full potentiality of their creative energies is to be actualized. Each of the two beings stands in a particular relationship to one of these principles, which is its own source of identity, its own *logos* and *sophia*, and which determines its destiny. The differentiation into male and female, far from being a compromise or a concession to human weakness, is intrinsic to the human state as such: it is a condition of the very existence of human nature itself.

This being the case, it may further be said that any endeavour on the part of man to transcend this differentiation through trying to regain what he supposes to be his original bisexual nature represents, not a step towards the perfecting of human nature, but a deviation from it. At best it is mere folly; at worst it is an attempt to go beyond the human norm and to aim at being God Himself. Such an attempt must meet with the fate that attends all such efforts to transcend the level of being on which and for which one is created, and in which one's perfection resides—the fate of which the fall of Lucifer is the paradigm. Consequently, any endeavour to suppress this differentiation and to achieve a state of sexual neutrality must also be seen as something that distorts or warps the being concerned, and prevents him or her from ever achieving the end for which he or she is created: his or her unique destiny as a human creature.

At least where the Christian tradition is concerned, the norm for what constitutes human life at its deepest and most radiant is provided by Paradise, the garden that God planted eastward in Eden, and by the two figures that inhabit it: a man and a woman, both created in the image of God, both created for immortality, yet each clearly to be recognized apart from each other by the predominance in them of the features and qualities, respectively, of masculinity and femininity, which they are to bear with them into eternity as ineradicable and inalienable features and qualities of their uniquely individualized beings. Each of them incarnates in a positive manner an aspect of the Divine; and any attempt on the part of either to deviate from, suppress or eliminate this God-given qualification, with the consequent loss or attenuation of masculinity in man and of femininity in woman, represents a step away from perfection and an obstacle to it. Both the bisexual person and the neutral person are parodies of the fully consummated human being.

Yet if the paradisal situation of man and woman is taken to provide the norm for human beings and an image of how such beings live when they live in accordance with nature and not contrary to nature, then something else of perennial significance is also to be noted. We have seen that, paradoxical as it may at first sight appear, God's self-determination on the human plane is most fully achieved in the creation, not of a single human being who embraces the principles of masculinity and femininity in himself, but of two individualized beings in each of whom respectively one of these principles predominates; and we have further seen that this predominance of either the masculine principle or the feminine principle is inextricably involved with the eternal destiny of both man and woman. That this is the case is re-affirmed in the Christian tradition by the recognition that Mary, the Mother of God, bears as fully the features and qualities of womanhood in her state of immortality, in which she is 'higher than the angels', as she did in her sojourn on the earth: no more in heaven than on earth can she by any stretch of the imagination be described as androgynous. Yet, in spite of the fact that she does not combine in her single being the principles of both masculinity and femininity, she has attained the supreme form of human perfection.

How, then, if this is the case, is one to explain what appears to be a discrepancy? When God created human nature in His own image, He created it male and female. Yet a person who most fully realizes the divine image and achieves the fullest likeness to God that can be attained by a human being does so without any loss or transcendence of sexual differentiation. Surely, it might be thought, whatever the order of things in the terrestrial sphere, this differentiation could be overcome when man attains the state of deification. How otherwise is one to envisage human nature in its totality as being *par excellence* the image of God if individual men and women cannot be other than predominantly male or female even after their deification? And will not individual men and women, even after their deification, be prevented otherwise from attaining anything more than one aspect of the fullness of the divine image and so to that extent always be in a state of destitution and self-exile, lacking the plenitude of reciprocity with the Divine which is bestowed on human nature by God when He brings it forth in His own image?

Yet if the paradisal situation is to provide the norm and model for human life and if in Paradise human nature, male and female in its integrity, is polarized into the individual masculine and feminine beings of man and woman, Adam and Eve, the full picture is still incomplete. For man and woman in Paradise, although independent identities each dominantly determined by complementary and even contradictory aspects of the Divine, do not lead their lives in isolation. They lead their lives *in relationship*. And it is precisely in this living of their lives in relationship that the mystery of God's bisexual nature is disclosed on the human plane in the most explicit manner. What neither man nor woman can attain as individuals living in isolation, they can attain through living in relationship. Concomitantly, it is in the relationship between man and woman, when this is lived in accordance with the norms of Paradise—under the conditions that apply prior to the fall into a state of forgetfulness and ego-centeredness—that the divine image is most fully achieved on the human plane and the divine archetype is made most fully manifest. For it is only in and by means of this relationship that the integrity of human nature, created male and female, is integrally represented on the human plane, and so is capable of conforming to the bisexuality of its archetype and of embracing fully both the masculine and the feminine principles. In other words, in their relationship Adam and Eve typify that primordial plenitude of human nature which each and all may emulate and attain.

This centrality of the relationship between man and

woman as the state which both discloses in the fullest possible way the ultimate mystery of divine life and provides, when properly understood and lived, the most propitious context for the perfecting of human nature itself, is re-affirmed in the Christian tradition by the fact that the divine-human event which lies at the heart of this tradition, and which constitutes the gage of its authenticity, take place within precisely such a context. It is not until Joseph takes Mary into his care, and Mary receives Joseph as her promised spouse, that the Holy Spirit makes His annunciation and the divine Logos is born in human form. Paradise may be entered, not tomorrow or after one's death, but here and now, provided one fulfils its conditions.

In that case, what are the conditions in accordance with which the primordial human relationship must be lived if it is to fulfil its positive role of bringing man and woman into the fullness of the divine image and so lead them to a state of perfection? The first thing to be said here is that it must be a relationship of love. This would seem to be so self-evident that it hardly requires any specification. Moreover, it is no more—even if no less—than a condition which should be fulfilled in all human relationships, not simply in that between man and woman. God is love; and in so far as we share in the divine image we also share in love and must express it in our activities. What more particularly characterizes the love between man and woman when this is manifest in their paradisal relationship—although the same will apply to its other manifestations—is the recognition that love itself is a divine quality and gift and does not belong to man in his own right. Thus when I say 'I love' I am really misappropriating something that is not mine, but which is expressing itself through me. This means that the distinction between sacred and profane love—the love that is paradisal and the love that is not—resides not so much in any qualitative difference in the nature of the love itself as in the qualitative difference in the consciousness of the sacred and profane lover. For the first recognizes that love is a divine quality and gift and responds to it accordingly, while the second, in the absence of such recognition, is liable to regard it as little more than an expression simply of his own ego, to use or abuse as he thinks fit.

Yet there is more than this. For if the lover recognizes that the love with which and in which he beholds the beloved is a divine quality, he will then be seeing the beloved in God. He will be seeing her in the light of the love that in its essence is divine. He will not be loving her therefore outside or apart from God. In the fallen state—or with the profane type of consciousness—it is quite possible for a man and a woman to love each other outside and apart from God, at least where their own awareness and intentions are concerned, and to see each other as beings that have no relationship with God and are quite independent of Him. But in the paradisal state, man and woman love each other in God, aware that it is only by being in God that they can love at all.

Nor is it simply in God that they love each other. For possessing as they do a spiritual form of consciousness they know that everything that exists is a self-articulation or self-revelation of the Divine. Everything is an unveiling of God, a theophany in which God discloses Himself in His own image. Hence in loving each other what they love is God as He has revealed Himself in each of them to the other. Each becomes an icon to the other; and because God has revealed Himself as an icon in the form of the living being who is the beloved, so in loving that being the lover will be loving God. In the icon it is God who manifests Himself; and what the man loves in the woman is the mystery she discloses as such an icon, just as what the woman loves in the man is the mystery that he discloses in a similar way. Each thus discloses for the other that unknown Being who is the sacred core of their existence and who Himself aspires to find a birthplace in the hearts of both of them. Nor is there anything idolatrous in this, for neither sees the other apart from or outside God.

Indeed, in this paradisal form of love between man and woman, the real lover—the real subject moving the love within the human lovers—is God Himself, the Lord of Love. The man and woman love God in each other not by or through themselves, but by and through God. Or, rather, in each it is God who loves the other. Such a love is physical, in so far as it is focused on and embraces an incarnate image. Yet it is also spiritual, since it does not want to possess the image but to be reborn in it and transfigured by it. What man and woman do in such a relationship is to invest each other with the concrete form of another living being who promotes in each the aspiration to grow towards the perfection for which both have been created. Their art—for it is an art to which they are committed—is to transfigure each other by arousing the full potentiality of their creative energies, bringing each other in this way ever more intimately into the presence of God. Seeing each other as the manifestation of the divine Beloved, the Lord of Love, they spiritualize each other's being by raising it beyond its physical or sensible form to its divine and incorruptible form, so that in the end their contemplation of God in each other becomes the highest form of contemplation of which human beings are capable, no less than that of God contemplating Himself in His own image.

It is in this way, then, and under these conditions that the relationship between man and woman fulfils its positive role of bringing them into the fullness of the divine image and likeness in which human nature is created and in which the divine archetype is most fully made manifest. Such a relationship can achieve this consummation because in it are engaged two beings each of whom enshrines aspects of the divine which the other only possesses in a rudimentary or stultified form. It should not be necessary to emphasize that it is not a case of man possessing a monopoly of male characteristics (whatever these may be), while the woman possesses a monopoly of female characteristics. What is in question is the predominance of certain aspects of the divine in each of the two, to such an extent that two totally non-interchangeable types of human being are produced. Thus it is possible to claim that while man is distinguished more by qualities of majesty and impartial judgment, woman is distinguished more by qualities of beauty and a sense of infinite tenderness and compassion. One might say that the corresponding differences are expressed in the natural world in the distinction between the mountain and the sea. At a deeper level man may be said to represent more the non-manifest creative energy of God and woman more the form in which God eternally reveals Himself to Himself, His manifest glory and the wisdom 'created before all things'; and this characterization of woman's prototype might be said to have its homologue in the natural world in the form of the sun through which the light of the sun is made manifest.

In this respect woman's prototype—the Eternal Feminine—enshrines the mystery of the divine Epiphany, for without the manifestation of His glory and His wisdom God's creative energy would remain unknown, unknowable, forever occulted, just as without the sun there would be no sunlight or without Mary the divine Logos would not have received a human form. Indeed, Mary is able to give birth to God in a human form only by virtue of the fact that on the transcendent spiritual plane her role as Mother of God is fulfilled by the Eternal Feminine, who eternally 'gives birth' to God; for only by symbolizing with her divine prototype could Mary fulfil her role on the human and temporal plane, the plane of history. Every divine revelation on the plane of history has its origin and prototype on the plane of metahistory, and is but a showing forth of the latter. In short, woman may be said to correspond more to the world of the Soul, not only in the cosmological sense, both as the 'place' in which God manifests Himself and as this manifestation itself, but also in an individual sense, as the aspect of each human being that projects itself on the imagination as a feminine form, the *Anima*. In her essence, she is 'the woman clothed with the sun', the Theotokos who is also the Theophany.

It should be repeated that this characterization of the differences between man and woman, however valid it is, does not in the least mean that man is destitute of the qualities present in a more marked fashion in woman, or *vice versa*. Nor do the differences in question imply any inequality between man and woman, for the prototypes of the qualities of which each is the manifestation and repository have no order of superiority and inferiority but are equally qualities of the divine Being who is their source. But to ignore such differences in the name of a misconceived egalitarianism is not only to do violence to the particular destinies that man and woman are called upon to fulfil but also, and *a fortiori*, to thwart the realization of the primordial human relationship of which we have been speaking.

It is in fact quite apparent that the realization of this relationship is only too often thwarted in the world of forgetfulness and separation in which for the most part we live. It is thwarted perhaps above all because what we have called the sacred or higher consciousness has been replaced by the profane or lower consciousness. When the sacred consciousness is operative—when, that is to say, in this relationship the man and the woman are both spiritually awakened—then it is in the woman that the man experiences human beauty as an epiphany of divine beauty, and it is in the man that the woman experiences in human form the majesty of God. Similarly with the other qualities which each possesses in a more marked manner than the other: it is in and through the other that each becomes capable of experiencing and integrating qualities which as separate individuals each of them lacks or has not developed.

Indeed, it is only by virtue of such an interchange of qualities that the relationship between them can grow into the fullness of the divine image and likeness. What makes a man and a woman not simply two isolated individuals each lacking aspects of the integrity of human nature, but two partners who together achieve human perfection, is what is added to each in and through their relationship, in and through what each bestows on the other. Moreover, this interchange of qualities operates in a way which as it were doubles each of them, since to the being of each as it is in and for itself is added the being of each as it is for the other. Hence in this relationship man and woman cease in a certain sense to be two individuals: they become four.

It is at this point that it becomes possible to grasp the true significance of the scriptural injunction (Gen 1:28), 'Be fruitful and multiply', announced by God to man when He first created man in His own image 'male and female'. Only too often literalist interpreters of Christian scripture—of whom, alas, there are far too many—take these words to mean that man and woman should produce children in the purely physical or corporeal sense, and indeed it is in this sense exclusively that man and woman are exhorted to 'be fruitful and multiply' in the marriage services of the Christian Church. How this conclusion is reached when it is clearly stated in the Book of Genesis that Adam knew Eve in the carnal sense only after their expulsion from Paradise and that it was only after expulsion from Paradise that they produced children 'according to the flesh', is something that these same interpreters tend to pass over in silence. One would have thought that if a stage towards human perfection is represented by man's return to the paradisal state, then the last thing one should exhort him to do is to function in a manner that both is symptomatic of and consolidates his fallen, non-paradisal condition.

In any case it is clear that if Adam and Eve produced any progeny in Paradise, they were of a kind different from those produced 'according to the flesh', and were begotten through a mode of intercourse other than the carnal mode. In addition, it might be asked how this literalist exhortation can be made to tally with one of the central Christian mysteries: that it was *after* Joseph took Mary into his care, but *before* he knew her in a carnal manner, that she conceived through the Holy Spirit and bore the Logos of God. This mystery should disclose for Christian partners a perspective quite other than that insisted on in their marriage services. However, this is but an only too typical example of how interpreters of Christian scripture tend, not to spiritualize the natural, but to naturalize the spiritual, thus consummating in their turn the original sin of Adam. The task of unravelling or resolving the contradictions and confusions that spring from this naturalizing of things of the spirit is one that those who must persist in perpetuating such a sin are the least likely to undertake.

The true significance of this scriptural injunction may be

approached by way of the Septuagint translation of the phrase in question. The words that in the English Authorized Version are translated as 'Be fruitful and multiply' are here translated into Greek as 'avxanesthe' and 'plithinesthe'; and of these Greek words the first is patent to the sense of 'grow' or 'become perfect', and the second to the sense of 'make full' or 'increase' not simply in a quantitative manner but also in a qualitative manner. Hence a translation from the Greek into English could read, not 'Be fruitful and multiply', but 'Grow to perfection and increase in spiritual fulness'—though it should be said in passing that no more than in western marriage services does the Orthodox marriage service stress this meaning of the phrase. Read in this light, the phrase accords perfectly with what has been said above about the mutual exchange of qualities in the love relationship between man and woman leading to human perfection and to growth into the fullness of the Divine.

Moreover, this interchange of qualities between man and woman can be seen as a mutual engendering and begetting that goes far beyond the begetting of children through the body. As Plato puts it, 'our nature longs to beget' (*Symposium*, 206C), and the engendering to which this leads is 'something ever-existent and immortal in our mortal lives' (*Symposium*, 206E), such generation being the only way through which we can attain the immortality in which our life is consummated (*Symposium*, 207D). But while some seek to achieve this immortality in an indirect manner through the begetting of children through the body, there are others 'whose creative desire is of the soul, and who conceive spiritually, not physically, the progeny which it is the nature of the soul to conceive and bring forth' (*Symposium*, 209A); and this generation is the generation of the spiritual or intelligible forms (of beauty, of love) with which God illumines the hearts of those who love Him. That is why the work of love may be described as 'to beget on what is beautiful by means of both body and soul' (*Symposium*, 206B), and why in the end the love between man and woman may be consummated in the vision of 'absolute beauty in its essence, pure and unalloyed' (*Symposium*, 211C).

The language is Platonic. But a vision similar to that which inspires it inspired likewise the language of many Christian authors in the mediaeval world. It must be remembered of course that the mediaeval world was one in which the Christian consciousness tended to be dominated by the male monastic and ascetic spirit in whose perspective earthly woman and feminine beauty as a whole feature, not as potential agents of transfiguring grace, but rather as temptations to be avoided at all cost, both in terms of outward social intercourse and in terms of meditation and the inward life. The condemnation and suppression of the role played by the *virgines subintroductae*[2] is perhaps typical of the spirit in question. It goes without saying therefore that the human relationship in which love is recognized to possess a redemptive and transfiguring power is for these authors not that between man and woman but that between man and man—not indeed in the erotic sense envisaged by Plato (still less in the modern homosexual sense), but in the sense of a deep spiritual friendship.

Hence there is no question of referring this relationship back to the paradigmatic paradisal relationship of Adam and Eve, so that its protagonists are seen to symbolize directly with the pre-fallen figures of the primordial human couple. Consequently, it cannot mirror the archetypal androgyny of the Divine with the same integrity as the relationship between man and woman. In this respect it must as a result fall short of fulfilling the plenitude of the divine image. Indeed, it may be said that, totally valid as it is in its own terms, the vision with which these mediaeval Christian authors invested the union of friends can only disclose its full potentiality when it is transposed to the relationship between man and woman.

For these authors,[3] friendship (*amicitia*) is not merely the highest form of human love. It is a divine manifestation, the revelation and communication of God Himself. St Augustine called his friend a unique revelation of God present within him. Hence to live in a state of friendship is to live in God or, as Aelred more succinctly puts it, friendship is God (*amicitia Deus est*). As such, friendship is a way of return to

Paradise, a means of raising oneself to God, of living in Him and of making Him live in us. Such a return to Paradise is seen as a new birth, a regeneration in God, a re-integration and a re-formation. It is the disclosure of a new heaven and a new earth, the revelation of the beatitude of those who dwell in heaven, an everlasting Sabbath, an entry, here and now, into the promised land and the New Jerusalem, an experience of the paschal resurrection, a return to the source of cosmic harmony and a reconciliation of opposites in an order of tranquillity, rest and peace. The unity of friends reflects the cosmic primal unity of all creation. For Aelred, the mere sight of a friend is a grace that leads one to recollection in God, and the joy of two friends is in God, but in God found and revealed in each other; while for Alcuin the very thought of a friend is like the visitation of the Holy Spirit that may be experienced through prayer. St Augustine sees the goal of the relationship between two friends attained in the union of their souls—or in what Cassian calls their forging of one heart and one soul in two bodies—in the possession of God, in their finding of one another in God.

Thus friendship is a profoundly religious experience, a hierophany or theophany at the heart of the Christian *mysterium*. To be united in love with the beloved is to find oneself returned to oneself, to one's full being. It is a re-attaining of one's paradisal wholeness, an association of the Holy Spirit. The paradise of a friend's love is a revelation of the divine Paradise, a transcending and a transfiguring of man's fallen and mortal state, a rebirth in God. As we have already remarked, the particular ethos in which this relationship of love is conceived and lived by these Christian authors of the mediaeval world restricted it to the association of man with man and hence it cannot fully symbolize with the archetype of the divine-human relationship, which is that of man and woman, Adam and Eve, through which the plenitude of the divine image is made manifest. But freed from this restriction and transposed to the relationship between man and woman, the vision that informs this love and the love that inspires this vision can realize their full potentiality.

That this vision has not, so far as one can tell, generally, informed the love between man and woman in the post-mediaeval western world is due partly at least to the fact that it has been so woefully eclipsed in the Christian consciousness itself. Yet only in its light can the relationship between man and woman be truly consummated. It should hardly be necessary to stress that such consummation can be attained only on condition that the partners concerned continuously and consciously refer what they receive and experience back to its divine source. They have to recognize that the gifts and graces with which they invest each other, and with which they are invested, are not their own and that they must not seek to possess them or to use them as a means to self-satisfaction or self-aggrandizement. For the vision that their relationship inspires in them would vanish as soon as they failed to acknowledge Who it is that consecrates their love and Whose love it is that validates their lives.

Yet it is some such failure of acknowledgement that results in the fall from the paradisal state of which the change in consciousness from the sacred to the profane is both the cause and the symptom. To some degree man begins to shift his focus and to see the centre of his being not so much in God, and in the corresponding spiritual essence in himself, as in his own ego and its proclivities. He begins to deny his ontological dependence on God and to seek to be the lord and master of creation in his own right. At the same time, and correspondingly, he is no longer capable of seeing the beauty of woman as an epiphany of divine beauty and to contemplate it in this way; he now wants to possess and appropriate it. His love becomes concupiscence and sensual covetousness, and the woman a separate phenomenon that he looks on as though outside and apart from God. Such covetousness places the human spirit in a negative sense beyond good and evil and in the end turns the love between man and woman into little more than a blind search to assuage ego-centred desires: carried along on an insatiable infernal current, man strives in vain to fill the bleak vacuity of his life by pursuing through successive hells unions which, being themselves chimerical, merely exacerbate the mental and moral disequilibrium of which they are the expression and of which he is the victim.

This process of profanation of which man is guilty has its counterpart also in woman. Indeed, if anything woman is even more prone than man to esteem things—including her own beauty—in terms of their sensory or aesthetic attraction, in terms of an amoralism and passion that do not take into account any spiritual or qualitative dimension. 'The woman saw that the tree was beautiful to eat, and that it was pleasant to the eyes to look on, and a tree to be desired . . . :' such was the disposition of Eve that led her to violate the divine commandment. Cut off in human consciousness from its roots in the Divine, and seen therefore as autonomous, beauty fascinates and destroys. The heavenly Aphrodite, betrayed into the streets and the market-place, assumes the terrible mask of the earthly Aphrodite. Woman becomes the seductress, and the relationship between man and woman an idolatrous cult, with little or nothing ennobling and transfiguring about it.

To say this is by no means to imply that all such relationships in our world are totally deprived of paradisal qualities. Every kind of tenderness, loyalty, endearment, cherishing and forgiveness engendered in the relationship between man and woman, as well as the exchange of physical delight, is an echo and intimation of the hidden beatitude man holds at the centre of his being. In this respect the heavenly Aphrodite may well reveal herself through the violations of her most abandoned earthly counterpart. But given the loss of consciousness of which we have been speaking, with our consequent failure to see things for what they are and to treat them accordingly, the relationship between man and woman does only too often fail to fulfil the role of which it is capable and which one might say constitutes its fundamental *raison d'être*, whatever other subsidiary purposes it may also serve. Only too often its potentiality is denied or frustrated. In a sense this is unavoidable so long as men and women think and act as though they were simply mortal and finite beings and forget they are immortal beings whose destinies cannot be fulfilled short of a realization of their spiritual nature. God is love, and like responds to like. How then can the God-given love between man and woman be brought to fruition if they fail to recognize and acknowledge the divine in each other? In other words, the failure to realize the full potentialities of this primal human relationship is made virtually inevitable by the hopelessly inadequate way in which man and woman regard each other, by their failure to recognize who they are and what their true reality is.

For when we do not see the need for putting down roots in the eternal, or when we deny that we have the capacity to do this, what we are actually doing is condemning ourselves and our activities to eventual disintegration. It is the harmony and rhythm of eternity that hold everything in its place and permit its growth; and whatever opposes this harmony and rhythm, or cuts itself off from them, will automatically disintegrate in the end through its inherent lack of reality. In spite of appearances, only that which comes from the source of life, and is directed towards the source of life, can possess reality in a true and enduring sense. The rest is but shadow-play, shadow despoiling shadow. Only that which puts down roots in the eternal can escape this process of mutual self-destruction, be sustained, and attain indestructability.

Man has not forfeited the divine image in which he is created, even if he fails to live and act in accordance with it. He can recover what he has lost. He can reverse the process by which he has reduced his consciousness to the level of profanity. But to do this he has to recognize that in essence he is a spiritual being whose deepest needs and aspirations can be fulfilled only through self-realization in God. Yet since God is love, this realization can be achieved only through the rebirth of divine love in his soul. Hence the crucial role in the whole process of regeneration or redemption that can and should be played by the nuptial relationship between man and woman. For the love they bear each other, and the longing for union which it promotes, are the expression both of their need and of their capacity to regain full consciousness of the beatific vision which they possess in the Paradise that lies within them: that vision in which they contemplate God in each other and which is fully manifest only in those in whom human love has been transfigured by the beauty of what they behold into a love that is itself divine.

NOTES

1. For a fuller discussion of this theme see my *Christianity and Eros* (London, 1976), pp. 51–74.

2. *Virgines subintroductae* is the name given to women who in the early Christian centuries lived in a state of spiritual marriage with men. The practice was forbidden by the canons of three fourth century Councils, although something analogous later characterizes the mixed monasteries of monks and nuns.

3. For a fuller account of this whole subject and for detailed references to all sources cited here, see: Mother Adele Fiske, '*Paradisus Homo Amicus*', in *Speculum*, July 1965, pp. 436–59.

9

VISION OF THE SACRED: THE CHOICE BEFORE US

✠

One of the factors that most inhibits our capacity to attain a vision of the sacred and hence to express it in our art is undoubtedly the ever-widening split in ourselves between our imagination—our intrinsic image-forming faculty—on the one hand, and our reason—our human instrument of discursive or logical thought—on the other. It might be said that, with scant exception, we tend to evade the issue of confrontation within ourselves between these two aspects of our consciousness. To put it another way—more apposite perhaps to the particular purpose of what follows—we tend to evade the issue of the dichotomy within ourselves between aesthetics or artistic expression, on the one hand, and metaphysics or theology (I use here the two terms as synonyms) on the other. In fact, to such a point has this dichotomy in us now developed that we are, quite literally, schizophrenic: the inner unity and harmony of our being are ruptured, we are self-divided, at odds with ourselves and consequently at odds with everything else as well.

This does not mean that we cannot in our time produce any art that is visionary, or that expresses intimations of the divine. That is not the case at all. But it does mean that so long as the dichotomy persists, whether in the person of the artist or in the disposition of his public, the odds are against our producing sacred art of the kind of which we recognize and acknowledge the magisterial beauty and power—and it is such art which surely must provide us with the norms of sacred art. Because a precondition of this art is precisely that there is no dichotomy between aesthetics or artistic expression, and metaphysics or theology. In other words, the split within ourselves which seems to grow ever wider is incompatible with the production of a fully articulated sacred art, whenever and wherever this is to be found. I will explain what I mean by this.

First of all, what exactly is meant by the term sacred art? A great deal of art—in fact most art worthy of the name—expresses intimations of the divine, aspirations for the divine, glimpses of the divine either in the human soul or in the world of nature. Is not created beauty itself, which after all is or should be a touchstone of art, always a reflection, an echo of the eternal beauty born at the beginning of things, however obscure or even distorted or misused its expression may be? Yet these qualities in a work of art do not in themselves make it a work of sacred art, just as references to God and the saints and so on in Engish hymns do not in themselves make these hymns works of sacred art. The quality that distinguishes a work of sacred art and that sets it apart from other works of art is I think one that can be described only by a word like knowledge, or gnosis.

Sacred art is a mode of knowing the Truth. It is a mode of knowing the Truth because it is the revelation of the Truth, its prophecy or its epiphany. Hence sacred art is not so much the expression of a human intimation of or aspiration for the Divine as the Divine itself revealing itself through the human. It is a gift of God of which the artist is the vehicle. It is an art, that is to say, that has its origin in the divine world and so can be produced only by those who have a knowledge or vision of that world. This means that before we can produce a work of sacred art we have to be in a position in which the realities of the divine world—sacred realities—can reveal themselves to us and permit us to know them; for clearly we cannot reveal these realities in our art until this has happened. Sacred art, then, is an attestation of the axiom, *Ars sine scientia nihil*—without knowledge there is no art—where the *scientia* or knowledge referred to is unambiguously knowledge of divine or sacred realities.

These realities that sacred art reveals are not abstract, static, impersonal or other-worldly. On the contrary, they constitute the inner living and energizing plexus of things, their inner being and identity. They are the spiritual archetypes whose intelligible ever-modulating metamorphoses from state to state link the Divine and the human, Creator and creation, from the most general to the most particular and intimate. It is this dynamic ever-modulating plexus that sacred art helps to reveal, to disclose and uncover.

In other words, sacred art presupposes that ours is a sacred cosmos rooted in the Divine and permeated to its very core by the unseen presence of divine powers whose actuality constitutes its own actual existence. But that there is this intimate interpenetration of inner and outer, invisible and visible, Spirit and matter, at work within us and in the world about us is not something that we can construe out of our own heads. It is something that can only be revealed to us by our own actual experience and perception of it. But before that can happen we have to recognize and accept not only that the cosmos does possess a sacred or spiritual dimension, and that this dimension constitutes its actual existence, but also that we possess the capacity to perceive and experience it; if we do not consciously recognize and accept this, both the true nature of the cosmos and our capacity to experience it will remain unknown, ineffective and unreal for us. If we do not first know what there is to see and experience, we will not even begin to cultivate the organs of vision through which we can see and experience it. It is the same as with any other potentiality: unless we become consciously aware that we actually possess it, we will not do anything about trying to realize it and to bring it to fruition.

How, then, do we first become consciously aware not only of the real nature of the cosmos but also of our capacity to experience it? The answer is that such knowledge is embodied in revealed sacred cosmology and sacred anthropology; and hence it is from such doctrine that we can learn in the first instance who we are and what is the real nature of things—learn, that is to say, in a theoretical sense, which is a precondition of knowing in an experiential sense. And by doctrine I do not mean dry-as-dust precepts formulated in academic council-rooms and committees. I mean the inspired utterances of prophets, sages, seers, poets: utterances, that is to say, of God Himself through which He reveals the magnificence and dignity, the sacramental homogeneity, of His own creation, in all its aspects. It is the nexus of such utterances, affirmed and re-affirmed in the lives of generation after generation of holy men and women, their immense meaning elucidated by masters of thought and language, that constitutes the principles of sacred metaphysical doctrine; and it is initially from such doctrine that, as I said, we can learn who we are—what we have the potential to be—and what constitutes the true nature of the cosmos.

Here I must make a short digression. What I have just stated—that the initial stage of coming to know God and the nature of the cosmos demands that we align our intelligence with the principles of sacred doctrine—may seem equivalent to putting ourselves into a strait-jacket, or at least to invading our freedom to a point that is unacceptable. Surely, it may be said, we can know God—know the Truth—or surely God may reveal Himself to us, quite apart from the recognition and fulfilment of a condition such as the one I posit? What does the phrase of Christ Himself—that the Spirit blows where He wills—mean if it doesn't mean this?

To answer such questions as they deserve is something that cannot be done here. But at least it may be said—and perhaps after all this is sufficient—that the New Testament phrase—the Spirit blows where He wills (John 3:8)—can be adduced to support the claim to such freedom only if it is taken completely out of its context and given an interpretation it does not and cannot bear. It does not mean that the Spirit—or God—acts or will act in relation to human beings quite apart from whether or not they fulfil certain specific conditions. It means that the Spirit—or God—is, unlike unregenerate man, a self-determining agent, and can Himself determine the conditions in which and according to which He acts. As is clear from the context, man himself, on condition that he is 'born of the Spirit', is then free to act in the same way—that is what the whole passage is about. But man can act as the Spirit acts only on condition that he is reborn in the Spirit; and to be reborn in the Spirit requires in its turn the fulfilment of certain other conditions.

It is totally sophistical to think that the Spirit—God—will reveal Himself to us, or allow us to know Him, and that we will be reborn in the Spirit, if we fail to fulfil those other conditions, and certainly this particular New Testament phrase gives no warranty for thinking that. On the contrary, God has testified endlessly through revelation direct and indirect, through apostles, saints, holy men and women, icon-painters and many others, to the conditions that have to be fulfilled before He wills—chooses—so to manifest Himself in human beings that they are reborn in Him, and, so far as I know, has given no indication anywhere that He will so manifest Himself if those conditions remain unfulfilled. One would not expect God quite to contradict Himself in that manner. In any case, if one appeals to this particular New Testament phrase in support of a particular viewpoint—even if one radically misinterprets it in the process—surely one should not ignore other statements on the same theme that come from the same source—statements such as that only the pure in heart can perceive or have vision of God and perceive sacred realities, which is a *sine qua non* of producing a work of sacred art.

To return to the main thesis: in the perspective of what I have said above it is clear that if there is to be an authentic sacred art then metaphysical knowledge and artistic expression must be intimately conjoined, for the sole purpose of both is and must be to reveal the Truth. In this respect the only difference between them is that in the case of metaphysics the Truth is expressed through symbols that are dominantly conceptual, while in the case of sacred art it is expressed through symbols that are dominantly imaginative. But whether it is our reason that conceptualizes the Truth, or our imagination that images it—iconizes it—there is and can be no dichotomy between what our reason conceptualizes and what our imagination iconizes: each supports the other, the images of our imagination are intelligible, the concepts of our reason are interpretable in terms of images, for our imagination and our reason run together, in the same harness.

They run together in the same harness because the

original act of vision on which both reason and imagination are dependent for their perception of the Truth is a noetic act: it is the act of the supreme cognitive faculty in man—what Yeats calls the spiritual intellect and Dante 'our noblest part, the part that most of all is the object of the love rooted in us':[1] a faculty that is to be radically distinguished from our reason in that it can directly apprehend the Truth—the spiritual archetypes of the celestial world—and is able to transmit its apprehensions in the case of the metaphysician to his reason, and in the case of the sacred artist to his imagination. The original organ of vision in both cases is the intellect; and if this noetic power is inactive or inoperative in us, then, even though we may acknowledge the principles of sacred metaphysical doctrine, we will still lack direct vision of the Truth that they enshrine; while if we do not acknowledge such principles, our imagination and reason may derive their images and concepts from other sources, but in that case what they produce or articulate will be neither sacred art nor a sacred doctrine.

Thus it can be said that a precondition of sacred art is that there is no split between our imagination and our reason, or between art and metaphysics: both are concerned with identical realities, and the only difference between them lies in the way they express these realities. As Dante—one of the greatest imaginations of Christendom—clearly puts it, with reference to the whole imaginative and symbolic unfolding of the *Divina Commedia*:

> *O voi che avete gl'intelletti sani,*
> *Mirate la dottrina che s'asconde*
> *Sotto il velame delli versi strani!*[2]
>
> You who have sound intellects
> Seek out the doctrine that conceals itself
> Beneath the veil of the strange verses.

If we now turn to look at our own situation we cannot but be aware that something drastic has happened. This intimate, inseparable bond between our imagination and our reason—art and metaphysics—is no longer effective.

Already in the second decade of the nineteenth century Keats can so conceive of the reason as something distinct from, if not opposed to, the soul, that he can speak of schooling the intelligence—here equated with the reason—to make a soul;[3] and before the century is out Yeats—albeit the young and immature Yeats—goes a stage further and speaks of attaining the new age, of which he regards himself as one of the pioneers, through a 'rise of soul against the intellect'[4]—the intellect here again equated with the reason. We tend to regard our reason as the great constraining force, something akin to Blake's Urizen, that for all practical purposes has ousted our imagination and bound us down into a false materialistic world. Correspondingly we tend to envisage our imaginative life, a life that thrives instinctively on myths and symbols—the kind of which sacred cosmologies are so full—as set over against the prison-house of our reason, for we have come to look upon these myths and symbols as essentially irrational, or at least beyond the scope of our reason. We tend to regard our imagination and our reason as more or less antagonistic, mutually incompatible, antithetical faculties, the one irreconcilably opposed to the other.

As a result of this we also tend to envisage artistic expression as demanding a revolt of our imagination against our reason. We have virtually been forced to affirm the autonomy of our imagination and its independence of our reason, and to claim that the images which it projects, insusceptible to rational explanation as they may be, none the less vehicle truths of an order that purely rational statements cannot elucidate. In this way we have developed an almost idolatrous attitude towards our imagination, regarding it as a law unto itself. Concomitantly we have come to look upon art as something essentially different from metaphysics, not simply in the way it expresses things but also with regard to what it has to express.

As a consequence we tend to esteem purely subjective imaginative and psychic states and intuitions as though they possess a quasi-sacred or sacrosanct character, as though their expression in art constituted a kind of sacred iconography, which need not be in the least intelligible, still less susceptible to any assessment or scrutiny on the part of our reason: there is no metaphysical doctrine that conceals itself beneath the veil of the poetry or the painting. Not only does it tend to be forgotten that our reason and our imagination are both faculties of our soul, so that for the one to be at odds with the other is tantamount to there being a state of civil war within our soul itself. We also tend to forget that both our reason and our imagination can function as organs through which the sacred reveals itself only on condition that both acknowledge the supremacy of the spiritual faculty in man—the spiritual intellect—which, according to all sacred doctrine, alone is endowed with the capacity to attain, under certain circumstances, a direct vision of the sacred. This means that the norms of sacred art are also disrupted, to such an extent that no sacred art in the full meaning of the words can be produced.

What is here being said involves basically two distinct questions. The first is: what is meant by saying that the human imagination can function as the organ through which the sacred reveals itself in the forms of art only on condition that it acknowledges and subserves the spiritual intellect? And the second is: how has it come about that the intimate relationship between art and metaphysics that typifies sacred art is by and large no longer effective for us?

To deal with the first question first. According to sacred doctrine,[5] the relationship between the imagination and the intellect is an articulation of the tri-partite structure of the universe or, rather, of a vision of things that posits three worlds, or rather, three categories of world. There is first the physical, sensory world, the world of phenomena that embraces our terrestrial world. There is then the suprasensory world of the soul, the world of symbolic images and figures and hence the world of the imagination in the universal sense of the word. And finally there is the celestial world, the world of pure Intelligences, most certainly not a world of concepts or abstractions, but a world of ever-living and ever-productive dynamic energies that constitute as it were the unmanifest seeds or the Divine Names in which all things have their origin, essence and true identity. These three worlds are accessible to man through corresponding organs of perception or cognition: the senses, the imagination and the intellect. And this triad in its turn corresponds to man's threefold structure, to the triad of body, soul and spirit, according to which man is not simply an earthly creature but possesses the capacity for resurrection in other worlds.

In speaking of the three categories of world in this way we are in danger of giving the impression that each is separate from and even independent of the others. This is not the case at all. They interpenetrate, each is inserted within the others. Thus, though the world of the imagination—and here and in what immediately follows I am speaking of the world of the imagination as a divine and universal category, not as pertaining to the individuated human soul—cannot be perceived by the senses (which does not mean that under certain conditions it cannot be perceived *through* the senses), yet each thing that has a sensory dimension has its analogue in the world of the imagination and these analogues are the image-archetypes of everything that exists in the visible world. Hence we can say that each thing we see is but the visible form of an invisible image-archetype, and manifests that archetype and is immanent in it, though the archetype is of a finer substance than the substance that composes its visible aspect.

Correspondingly, this invisible psychic dimension of each living physical thing—the image-archetype of each visible reality, or its angelic nature—is itself the unfolding and psychic flowering of a still deeper or more interior reality, the spiritual seed or Divine Name of which the psychic reality is itself but the image; and it is the spiritual reality of each living existence that constitutes its true and innermost identity, its eternal being and reality, that constitutes the truly sacred dimension of both the psychic and the physical world as of every individual and singular thing that the psychic and physical worlds embrace. And just as the image-archetypes of the world of the imagination cannot be perceived by the senses, so this spiritual and sacred dimension of things cannot be perceived by the imagination: it can be perceived and known only by the organ of perception in man that corresponds to it, and this organ is the spiritual intellect.

Yet at the same time, just as each thing we see is but the visible form of the image-archetype of the world of the imagination in which it is immanent, so the whole psycho-physical—soul-body—reality of each thing is the manifestation of the spiritual and sacred reality that constitutes its true and eternal identity and being, and it is immanent in this reality, as it were ensheathed by it. The psycho-physical reality of each thing, that is to say, is immanent in the spiritual reality that it manifests, just as the physical reality of each thing is immanent in the psychic reality that it manifests. There is no split, no dualism of Spirit and matter in reality itself.

Thus in this scheme of things the world of the imagination possesses an intermediary and mediative place and role. It occupies an ontologic level that is above the sense-world but below the world of spiritual archetypes, more immaterial than the first, less immaterial than the second. Thanks to this position, it is the world through which the divine essences of things are transmuted into their corresponding exterior forms, and also through which the exterior physical forms of things are spiritualized or resurrected: through which what is spiritual assumes a body and what is corporeal becomes spirit. This is why everything in the physical world, from the most general to the most particular and intimate, is an epiphany or showing-forth of the world of the imagination—an epiphany or showing-forth of the image-archetypes embraced by the world of the imagination.

Yet these image-archetypes of the world of the imagination themselves constitute the epiphany—or one might here more positively say the theophany—of the divine essences or Divine Names that are embraced by the level of reality that ontologically precedes the world of the imagination. This level of reality is the celestial world of the spiritual Sun or fount of all things: the world in which God initially reveals Himself to Himself in the light of His own Wisdom.

It should now be clear why the human imagination must

be dependent on the spiritual intellect if it is to participate in the vision of the divine essences of things whose exteriorization either in the forms of living creatures or in the forms of art constitutes the epiphany of the sacred. For the power through which this vision is effected is a noetic power. It is the power of the intellect, the organ in man that alone is capable of direct apprehension or perception of divine realities. If this organ is inactive or inoperative, the human imagination may fill itself with images from other sources, but it cannot become pregnant with the seeds of the celestial world. As a result it cannot give birth in itself to the image-archetypes that are truly epiphanies of the celestial world and that may therefore be termed sacred. Consequently it cannot produce forms of art that possess a sacred quality.

In the light of this it is not difficult to see where our increasing reluctance, and even inability, to recognize that a condition of producing a work of sacred art, in the full sense of the words, is that the artist has to school his imagination to acknowledge and subserve the spiritual intellect, and hence a sacred metaphysical doctrine, must lead and has led. It is not that we have repudiated the idea of expressing sacred realities in works of art. It is more that the terms on which we think that this can be done have radically changed. We do not think that the artist has to work hand in hand with a metaphysical or theological doctrine, or that his task is to affirm a sacred cosmos. We do not think that the human imagination, in order to function as the vehicle of the sacred, must conform itself to the vision of a superior faculty, the spiritual intellect.

On the contrary, we tend to regard our imagination as itself our supreme visionary faculty, whose full deployment is or can be—even should be—quite independent not only of our reason but of the spiritual intellect as well, in fact we tend to make no distinction between the two faculties, and to regard metaphysical or theological discourse as essentially non-imaginative and anti-visionary. It is virtually taken for granted that the kind of truth revealed through the human imagination, and hence through art, is totally different from and superior to the kind of truth articulated by our reason. Correspondingly, it tends to be forgotten that our imagination can be just as deluded as our reason—that the devil can play tricks equally with both—so that the assumption that what comes from it in the forms of art is automatically sacred is plain wishful thinking, if not worse. We do not appear to realize that the pursuit of visionary experience not synthesized with a fully articulated sacred doctrine, cosmological and anthropological, is just as likely to terminate in hallucination, dementia and disintegration as the pursuit of philosophy uninspired by visionary experience is to degenerate into the kind of sterile logic-chopping and vain speculation that characterizes so much that goes by the name of philosophy at the present time.

In fact we do not appear to realize that if the artist—or anyone else for that matter—deliberately or accidentally invokes the spiritual archetypes without having made his own the intelligence and purity that is theirs in the celestial world, and for motives and purposes inconsistent with that intelligence and purity, he will experience them as unsubdued, spectral and full of horror; and he will automatically become the prey of their uncontrolled and destructive emanations and be transformed into their terrible likeness. Such was the fate of Mr Kurtz in Conrad's *The Heart of Darkness*; and such a state of soul is shown forth in much contemporary art, whether music, poetry or painting. The notion that the paradigms of sacred art, however pure in their original state, cannot, on their passage towards materialization, be subverted in the human soul into vehicles for transmitting an infernal influence is a dangerously false one.

This brings us to the second of the two questions posed above: how has it come about that by and large we regard our imagination and our reason as antithetical faculties? How have we become victims of a dichotomy within ourselves between aesthetics, or artistic expression, and metaphysics or theology?

The answer to this question, in a nutshell, is that, quite literally, we have been brainwashed; and the history of how this abnormal state of affairs has arisen—of how the choice for most of us now is between betraying the great themes of human spirituality or opting out for the trivialities of our own ego—is the history of our brainwashing. As remarked in the opening chapter of this book, an initial stage in this process—it can be traced back to the mediaeval scholastic philosophers—was to make a distinction between two kinds of knowledge, or two kinds of knowing. There is the knowledge of the sphere of metaphysics or theology—of eternal and supranatural realities—and this is the effect of faith; and there is knowledge of the sphere of temporal and natural realities, and this is the effect of the reason. Theoretically there could be no disagreement or contradiction between these two types of knowledge, because both the eternal and the temporal, the supranatural and the natural, have a single author, God; and God cannot contradict Himself. But as metaphysical or theological criteria and principles were pushed more and more into the background, so they were regarded as more and more irrelevant where knowledge of temporal and natural realities—of the created cosmos—was concerned. Correspondingly, where the knowledge of the created cosmos was concerned, criteria and norms other than those enshrined in sacred doctrine and sacred cosmologies became increasingly effective, to such a degree that in the end they entirely displaced those of metaphysical or theological doctrine.[6]

Yet at the same time, because the knowledge of the sphere of the temporal and the natural was said to be the effect of the reason and therefore a rational knowledge, these criteria or norms—the premisses—according to which this knowledge was now determined were themselves regarded as rational. This knowledge is of course the knowledge of modern science—and by modern science I mean the science that issued from the philosophical revolution of the sixteenth and seventeeth centuries, the premisses of which no scientist has yet repudiated, let alone replaced; so that what I am here saying is that it is the premisses governing modern science that are now regarded as rational. Modern science comes to be esteemed as *par excellence* a rational science, the science of the reason. Its hard facts are rational facts. Indeed, bit by bit modern science is credited with possessing a monopoly of the reason. Anything that contradicts it—at least with respect to the sphere of the world of phenomena—is consequently regarded as non-rational, or irrational, which is tantamount to saying that it is non-sensical.

This might not have mattered had the premisses effective for the modern scientific mentality coincided with those effective for sacred metaphysical or theological doctrine. But unfortunately this is not the case: they are entirely different. Consequently the images of reality—the world-pictures—to which they give birth are also entirely different. And because modern science is regarded as essentially a rational science, it is the world-picture of modern science—now radically different from the world-picture of sacred cosmology—that is regarded as the rational world-picture. As a result sacred cosmology—the kind of cosmology that underpins Dante's *Divina Commedia* as it underpins Chartres cathedral, or the Taj Mahal, or the wall-paintings of Ajanta or the Constantinopolitan Church of St Saviour in Hora, or the music of India or of the great Tudor masters—this kind of cosmology, because it does not accord with the norms of modern science, is on that account regarded as non-rational, irrational, and hence as purely imaginary in the sense of being purely unreal.

Yet the process does not stop with the norms of modern science being regarded as the only ones competent to assess the truth of things in the visible, physical cosmos. These norms have come to be regarded as capable of assessing the significance of things in the world of the soul as well. The whole world of the psyche is invaded by the modern scientific mentality, which arrogates to itself the prerogative of explaining to us the meaning of the events and processes that go on in the world of the psyche. And as the world of the psyche is the world of myths and symbols—such as are embedded in sacred cosmologies and constitute the natural nourishment of the aspiring sacred artist—this mentality presumes to explain to us the significance and meaning of these myths and symbols as well. They, too, become subject to what is still considered to be the unquestionable objectivity of the scientific reason. As for what I have called the celestial world, the world of pure intelligences that are in fact the shaping, motile, sustaining and consummating powers of both psychic and physical worlds, doctrines concerning this world are adroitly manipulated and subverted to accord with the hypotheses that the modern scientific mentality accepts as axiomatic.

The repercussions of all this could not be other than disastrous, no less than that split in our consciousness between our imagination and our reason which is reflected in the further split between art and metaphysics. In fact we have been forced into a totally abnormal and self-defeating either-or position. Either we can accept the validity of the world-view of modern science, as well as what follows from it—and if we accept its rationality we can hardly deny its validity—and regard it as the task of art to 'poeticize' the world which this view would have us believe is the real world. Or we can still attempt to keep faith with the world of the imagination in the universal sense, and allow our imaginations to gravitate towards their natural lodestones, the image-archetypes of the psychic world, and to use their symbolic forms and figures in our art. But in so doing either we are not wanting to affirm the sacred or sacramental nature of the cosmos at all because we think that the modern scientific understanding of the cosmos, desacralized and neutralized as it is, is none the less a rational and hence a valid kind of understanding; or if we do wish to affirm the sacred or sacramental nature of the cosmos we are forced—short of challenging the modern scientific view on its own ground, the ground of reason—to affirm it in spite of the reason and in terms, as I said before, of a revolt of our imagination against our reason.

It is this latter course that poets in the Romantic tradition have tended to take. They do not presume to challenge the modern scientific view on its own ground—that of reason—because on the side of reason they are now totally disarmed: like more or less everybody else they have capitulated to the belief that the scientific view of things is a rational view, at least where the knowledge of the physical world is concerned. Consequently, when they attempt—in spite of what their reason now accepts—to express in conceptual terms a view of things that is essentially non-scientific (in the modern understanding of the word), the statements that they make appear to be forced upon the poetry instead of growing out of it, and in this respect to be quite arbitrary and rhetorical, and even in some cases simply erratic. One has only to think of statements as familiar as Keats's

> 'Beauty is truth, truth beauty,'—that is all
> Ye know on earth, and all ye need to know

to see what is meant by this. Although Keats himself may well have based this affirmation on his reading of Plotinus—some would say on his misreading of Plotinus—not only is it not organically supported by the context and bent of the poetry itself, but it comes as a kind of *deus ex machina* that taken at its face value can only lead, as in fact in the latter half of the nineteenth century and subsequently it did lead, to what has been called[7] the most horrible putrefaction in both life and art.

Or there is Shelley's

> Life like a dome of many-coloured glass
> Stains the white radiance of eternity

—again a statement that Shelley himself may have believed was based on sound Platonic or Neoplatonic doctrine, but one which again, in the context of the poetry itself, appears to be purely rhetorical—indeed hardly to qualify as poetry at all. What it seems to represent is simply the assertion of the frustrated and disinherited will trying to outstrip the unimaginative and unimaginable categories of modern science; but in the event it fails to explain anything, because in terms of what the reason now accepts as defining the truth of things explanations of this kind are virtually meaningless.

To illustrate this more clearly one has only to contrast such conceptual statements as those just quoted with the way in which, for instance, Shakespeare, in whom imagination and metaphysics run together, quite naturally invokes in what might otherwise appear to be a purely descriptive passage the most profound intelligible meaning—a meaning consecrated by the wisdom of sacred cosmology. Examples are rife; but one may take to illustrate the point the passage in which Macbeth adjures the witches to answer him, even if all hell is let loose as a consequence.[8] Among the list of possible disasters that he is willing to risk being unleashed is the tumbling together of Nature's germens—

> though the treasure
> Of Nature's germens tumble all together
> Even till destruction sicken

The phrase may sound strange to our ears, but clearly to Shakespeare and his audience it did not. Yet it is a phrase that refers directly back to the Neoplatonic and Christian doctrine of the *logoi spermatikoi* or *rationes seminales,* those invisible seeds or seminal causes—the divine essences or exemplars or ideas—of which visible things are the expression and the embodiment.[9] That such a cosmological doctrine could still be invoked without producing embarrassment or scorn is testified by the fact that it can form the substance of a conceit in a simple love lyric, as it does in Carew's 'These flowers as in their causes sleep'.

It might be protested that more specifically religious poets of the last century or so like Hopkins or T. S. Eliot do close the gap between imagination and metaphysics, and as a consequence do produce a poetry that may be called sacred in the true sense of the words.[10] Hopkins certainly gave his adherence to a religious doctrine—a kind of romanticized Scotism compounded with Cardinal Newman's anti-intellectualism—and intended that his poetry should be a vehicle for expressing it. But in fact the poetry fails to do this. The kernel of Hopkins' theology is that what he calls the 'Ground of being, and granite of it'—the essential being of all natural things—is no less than Christ, or Christ-as-sacrifice; and in the poems in which he attempts to convince us of this he gives us a glittering spate of images in which he senses or intuits the divine presence in the visible world.

Yet when it comes to the point, what time and again Hopkins' religious poetry does is to assert a theological conclusion that in itself is external to the intuitive images of the poetry, does not arise out of them and is not verified or validated by them; and the consequence is that in the end the poetry fails to show us what it professes or attempts to show us. An image whose purpose is to convey an intuition cannot also serve to convey a theological or metaphysical conclusion; and yet this is what Hopkins demands that it should do, for the meaning he wants to convey is that natural things body forth the beauty of Christ and that precisely is a theological meaning. An intuition simply as an intuition cannot do the work of a theological concept. Hopkins' poetry, for all its brilliance and ecstatic language, does not fulfil the role of sacred art. It does not and cannot reveal to us that ours is a sacred universe.

Nor does Eliot's poetry fulfil that role. It might be said that Eliot does not even intend that it should fulfil it, at least in the way that Hopkins attempted to make his poetry do so, by presenting the world to us as a theophany. Eliot's world—his cosmos—is thoroughly neutralized: natural things are simply natural things, and there is little or no intuitive apprehension of God as the being of things, still less any transfiguring of the material into the spiritual, the physical into the metaphysical. Though the poetry deliberately arouses theological and cosmological expectations, there is no framework of thought and symbol within the poetry itself through which these expectations can be answered. As a result, such metaphysical or theological phrases as 'the still point of the turning world' are simply left dangling, uninterpretable within the context of the poetry itself, and interpretable only in the sense that your guess is as good as mine. Once again, the meaning is missed, whatever the experience might have been. No doubt both Hopkins and Eliot had the disposition that Dante had to integrate the experience with a complete rationale of things, theological and cosmological; but Dante possessed such a rationale, and they did not—above all did not precisely in relation to that cosmological vision that Shakespeare or Carew could invoke in a single phrase existing quite naturally within the poetry itself.

In other words our reason, cut off from its roots in metaphysical or theological doctrine, can no longer underpin and support our imagination; while our imagination, deprived of this support and at the same time affirming what amounts to its autonomy and certainly its independence of the spiritual intellect, cannot fulfil its sacred task of transmuting either spiritual realities into the forms of art or, still less, of transmuting, with the assistance of art, the physical world—of transfiguring and resurrecting things by revealing their sacred identity to them and to us. The reality of sacred myth and symbol, grounded in metaphysical knowledge, and the reality of what are now regarded as the rational facts that constitute knowledge of the physical cosmos, have fallen so far apart that the one has virtually nothing to do with the other. 'What's water but the generated soul?' asks Yeats, affirming the vision of sacred cosmology; and what else indeed is it? But how can we actually, and not just romantically or rhetorically, know and experience it like that—know and experience the true miracle of water—when our reason tells us that water is nothing but two parts hydrogen and one part oxygen? With the best will in the world the schizophrenia is too great to be endured—it is a tightrope act demanding the impossible. And we are simply deluding ourselves if we think otherwise. It was Oscar Milosz who said that we cannot actualize our spiritual potentiality, let alone produce a sacred art, unless and until the inner spiritual vision we have of things is in harmony with the way in which we actually conceive, rationally and consciously, and perceive the outer physical world.

As it is, schooled as most of us are from the word go to conceive and perceive the outer physical world in ways shorn virtually of the last vestiges of sacred vision, it is only by what one might call providential intervention that we even begin to recognize and accept that our comos is, or may be, a sacred cosmos; while to translate this incipient recognition or acceptance into living knowledge and experience, so that it can impregnate and vitalize the forms of our art, may take half a lifetime or more, requiring as it does that we have to unlearn practically everything we have been educated to think and to feel. It was only at the end of his life that a poet so richly endowed, and so assiduous in metaphysical study, as Yeats managed to break through into the kind of vision that poets like Kabir, or Rumi, or Dante, could accept as their natural heritage and birthright. The situation of anyone seriously concerned with the pursuit of spiritual vision in our age can fittingly be compared to that of a whale trapped beneath an icepack and having to expend the greater part of its energy in swimming against the intolerable current simply to keep itself beneath the airhole on which its respiration, and hence its life, depend. In such a situation it is hardly surprising that in our age the kind of art inspired by spiritual vision is the exception rather than the rule.

What, then, is the choice before us? I said that the history of how this abnormal state of affairs has come about is the history of our brainwashing, of a gigantic hoax. What exactly do I mean by this? My thesis—or a crucial part of it—is that we get an authentic sacred art only when our imagination works hand in hand with sacred metaphysical doctrine, and particularly with those cosmological and anthropological aspects of such doctrine that affirm the sacramental nature of creation. But that means that our imagination has also to work hand in hand with our reason, for it is our reason that gives assent to such doctrine and to its consequences where our understanding of the nature of the cosmos is concerned.

Yet here precisely is the rub. For we have been persuaded that the world-picture of modern science is a rational one because we have been persuaded that modern science is a rational science: that in fact is why we have given our assent to the world-picture it has produced. That being the case, we cannot expect our reason to assent simultaneously to a view of the cosmos that is, as I said, diametrically opposed to this. We cannot ask it to assent to a sacred cosmology and to all that that implies.

It is, however, precisely what one might describe as the sleight of hand through which we have been persuaded that modern science is a rational science, and that consequently its cosmology is a rational cosmology, that constitutes what I have called a hoax but might equally have called a demonic possession. We have literally allowed our reason to be kidnapped by a set of premisses—a framework of concepts or assumptions—whose truth can in no way be established by the reason and which, moreover, are, from the point of view of metaphysical doctrine, completely fraudulent. I will explain what I mean.

The reason can function only on condition that it accepts, consciously or unconsciously, a set of premisses—a framework of concepts or assumptions—that provide it with a starting-point or with starting-points from which to function and according to which it continues to function. Such premisses constitute the norms effective for it, and in obedience to which it operates. But in themselves these premisses are not and cannot be the product of our reason: clearly our reason cannot itself produce the premisses whose acceptance by it is a condition of its being able to function in the first place. On the contrary, they pre-empt our reason, they set our reason to work for them, and without them our reason would remain inert, inoperative. They are simply concepts, or assumptions to which our reason gives its assent as a condition of being able to think logically and rationally at all.

Our reason, then, functions within the context of a set of premisses to which, consciously or unconsciously, it has given its assent. This set of premisses determines the conclusions that it reaches as a result of its reasoning. These conclusions will be rational conclusions only in so far as they are logical deductions from the premisses in question, only in so far as one proposition follows logically from another. But that these conclusions are logical deductions from their premisses in no way establishes their truth or validity: their truth or validity will depend entirely on the truth of their premisses, on the degree to which these premisses do in fact correspond to the reality of things. And the degree to which these premisses do in fact correspond to the reality of things is something that it is entirely beyond the competence of our reason itself to assess. Indeed, the notion that by its own unaided light the human reason is capable of assessing the truth of things in either the physical or the intelligible order is a totally fallacious notion.

This does not in the least mean that we are trapped in a hopeless kind of relativism, in which what one person thinks is as good as what any other person thinks. But what it does mean is that my assent to a particular set of premisses presupposes an act of faith: I have to acknowledge my belief in it. In other words, if modern science possesses no monopoly of reason, religion possesses no monopoly of faith. Reason and faith have equivalent roles where both are concerned, for it is an act of faith in either case that commits me to their premisses, and it is this commitment that gives my reason its mandate to function in their name. What initial act of faith I make is entirely at my own discretion. But if I am to think at all, one thing I cannot escape: I cannot not derive the premisses according to which I think from somewhere. And if I do not derive them from sacred doctrine, and they differ from those of sacred doctrine, the least I can do is to try to be aware of the source from which I do derive them, and of what they consist, and why that is my choice. The notion of free thought is one of the more stupid inventions of the iconoclastic mind—almost as stupid as the notion, so common today, that you can reject one form of doctrine—one form of dogmatic orthodoxy—without embracing some other form.

Our brainwashing therefore—to return to my theme—consists not in the fact that we have been persuaded that the findings of modern science follow rationally from their premisses—they do so follow—but in the fact that we have been persuaded that these premisses in themselves are rational premisses in the sense that they can be verified by the reason, and that it is on account of this that modern science is a rational science. We have allowed our reason to be kidnapped by these premisses, to work for them, and to deduce conclusions from them, as though they were objectively valid and true, as though they did correspond to the reality of things, even in fact as though they were self-evident. It is in their name that we have desacralized the world, demythologized and depersonalized it in our consciousness, and it is in their name that we have rejected the sacred cosmologies as basically untrue and fictitious, and have substituted for them a cosmology or cosmologies as remote from them as it or they possibly could be. And yet, as

I said, the truth of the premisses of this cosmology or these cosmologies can in no way be established by the reason: it is simply not susceptible to rational demonstration. And the premisses themselves are anything but self-evident.

Where, then, does this leave us? First it frees us from the illusion that modern science is a science based on rational premisses in the sense specified and that consequently the statements made in its name about the nature of man and of the world in which he lives are *ipso facto* rational statements. In fact it frees us from the illusion that the period dominated by the kind of philosophy that typifies the modern scientific mentality constitutes the Age of Reason and that people whose reason subserves this kind of philosophy, and all its offshoots, are therefore rationalists, while people whose reason subserves metaphysical or theological doctrine are not: there never has been, and never can be, an Age of Reason, just as there never have been, and never can be, coherent thinkers who are not rationalists. Second, it frees us from the illusion that if we give our assent to the principles of a sacred cosmology we are thereby committing ourselves to a view of the world that is essentially irrational, non-scientific, and hence non-sensical. And, third, it means that if we do commit ourselves to the principles of a sacred cosmology—and this we have to do before there can be any question at all of any aspiration to a renewal of sacred art that is not entirely futile—we have not only to affirm that these principles are true in the sense that they truly correspond to the reality of things; we have also to affirm that the premisses of modern science are untrue—are fraudulent and spurious—in the sense that they do not correspond to the reality of things: in this respect, as in many other respects, we cannot eat our cake and have it.

For if the principles of sacred cosmology do correspond to the reality of things, and if the cosmology, or cosmologies—the world-pictures—proposed by modern scientists are radically at odds, as they are, with sacred cosmology, it must follow that the premisses underlying these modern scientific cosmologies do not correspond to the reality of things. It must follow that the starting-points of the modern scientific thought-processes which produce these cosmologies are at odds with the principles of sacred doctrine, that they do not accord with revelation or with any tradition of holy wisdom. In other words it must follow that they are completely arbitrary starting-points, figments of human thought or mere assumptions the ultimate ground of whose relevance is totally unknown and even illusory. And if the ultimate ground of the starting-points of one's thought is totally unknown and even illusory, and the intermediate steps in one's reasoning are consequently also based upon what is totally unknown and even illusory, it is quite clear that the resulting conclusions cannot be anything that by any manner of means can possibly be said to constitute knowledge.

This can be illustrated in more concrete terms by referring to what from the metaphysical point of view is a major fallacy embedded in modern scientific epistemology. A cardinal assumption of this epistemology is that it is possible to obtain a knowledge of physical realities without a prior knowledge of metaphysical realities. The validity of this assumption itself depends of course upon the validity of another assumption, namely that there is a world of purely physical realities so independent of metaphysical realities that it is possible to obtain a knowledge of it without possessing a prior knowledge of those metaphysical realities. But such an assumption cuts right across the metaphysical perspective of sacred cosmology, according to which physical realities are the manifestation—the epiphany—of metaphysical realities and apart from them could have no being and no reality whatsoever.

This means that in the metaphysical perspective there can be no knowledge of physical realities that is not entirely dependent on a prior knowledge of metaphysical realities. And it further means that in this perspective you cannot obtain a knowledge of the physical world on the assumption that the physical world is so independent of metaphysical realities that such a knowledge is a possibility; for this assumption presupposes that you have in your mind already abstracted the physical world from what in fact constitutes its being and reality, and hence that what you are trying to obtain a knowledge of is a pure abstraction that possesses no reality other than that attributed to it by the mind that conceives it or assumes it. From this point of view, therefore, the assumption described above as a cardinal assumption of modern scientific epistemology is based upon an illusion, that is to say on a conception of things that does not correspond to their reality; and clearly, as already remarked, conclusions whose starting-point is based on illusion cannot possibly be said to constitute knowledge.

We must be quite clear about what is here being said. There has in recent years been much talk of reconciling modern science and religion, much talk of trying to integrate this science with some kind of metaphysics, to latch it on to Christian doctrine, or to Taoism, and in this way to give its most cherished theories—the theory of evolution, or of relativity, or the quantum theory, and so on—some kind of religious status. But it must be remembered that these modern scientific theories about the nature of the cosmos have themselves been arrived at not only quite apart from any prior commitment on the part of their authors to sacred metaphysical doctrine, but also on the assumption that one can obtain a valid knowledge of the physical world by examining it as though it were independent of the metaphysical world. As a consequence, every attempt to fit these theories into the context of metaphysical doctrine has meant, and inevitably must mean, buckling metaphysical doctrine so that it can accommodate what are in fact, from the metaphysical point of view, pure lies; for from the metaphysical point of view no true knowledge whatsoever of the physical world can be acquired as a result of examining it as though it were something entirely other than what it is.

This last affirmation applies also with reference to what one might call the last ditch stand of the modern scientific establishment. Here it is not claimed that there can be a reconciliation between religion and modern science. Rather it is claimed that there is no need to make a clear-cut, either-or choice between serving the premisses effective for the modern scientific mentality and serving those of sacred metaphysical doctrine: one can assent to both. One can assent to both because although the norms of sacred doctrine may be appropriate where spiritual and imaginative realities are concerned, this is not the case where the physical reality of things is concerned: knowledge obtained through applying the norms effective for modern science is quite valid on its own level. Thus even if the general theories extrapolated from the facts ascertained as a result of analysing phenomena according to the modern scientific method may be hypothetical and hence open to question, the facts themselves are not hypothetical and are not open to question: water consists of two parts hydrogen and one part oxygen, and that is that.

Yet to argue in this way is simply to proclaim oneself still a victim of what one might call, if not the original sin, at least the original symptom of the dichotomy with which we are afflicted: victims of that false philosophy which would have us acknowledge that the sphere of metaphysics or theology is one thing and that the sphere of nature is another, and that consequently we can ascertain the facts of nature without any reference to the facts of the metaphysical world. It is forgotten, or left unspecified, that the mind which analyses phenomena according to the method that produces the so-called facts of modern science is a mind already committed to assumptions about the nature of these phenomena and the propriety of certain procedures, mathematical and other, for obtaining an objectively valid knowledge of them, that from the metaphysical point of view preclude any notion of them that is not radical misrepresentation. From this point of view, therefore, so-called modern scientific knowledge is not only non-knowledge; it is also duplicity. It does not apply to the things to which it purports to apply. It applies only to what a particular type of human mind—one committed to a particular set of assumptions—is able to perceive of these things after it has abstracted them from their reality or evacuated their reality from them.

In short, if we commit ourselves to the principles of a sacred cosmology we have to affirm that once our reason has lost its anchorage in sacred doctrine or noetic vision it is exposed to the kind of delusion that corresponds to that to which our imagination is exposed in similar circumstances: it is exposed to becoming the prey of assumptions dreamed up by some totally disorientated mind or minds, promoted by God knows what influences and interests, and plausibly insinuated into the structures of school, university and other mechanisms of mass propagation and persuasion until they completely displace the principles of holy wisdom. In terms of our local European history—which threatens to become world history—the counterfeit norms that above all have displaced the principles of holy wisdom, and of which the reason has become the prey, are those that underlie the emergence and domination of the modern materialist scientific view of things. One might say that far from constituting an Age of Reason, or of Enlightenment, the period—which includes our own times—characterized by the ascendancy of this view of things constitutes an age of the most benighted and bleak form of idol-worship and ignorance.

The choice, then, that we have to confront if we wish to see any renewal of sacred art—in fact, if we wish to continue to exist at all—is first of all that of freeing our reason from its captivity to the counterfeit norms—the false premisses—that have produced this modern scientific view of things, and simultaneously of rooting it in the principles of sacred doctrine. And should it be protested that this is simply the equivalent to taking our reason out of one strait-jacket and putting in into another, it must be replied that there is all the difference in the world between being shackled by the mind-forged manacles of a philosophy that is a purely human invention and being liberated from such manacles by the God-given intellectual symbols of eternal wisdom.

Not only is there absolutely no need for any revolt of our imagination against our reason, but to act as though there is is simply further to consolidate the present dichotomy in our consciousness, our present state of self-division and schizophrenia. What on the contrary is needed is a revolt on the part of our reason itself against its servitude to that whole way of thought which increasingly over the last centuries has estranged our reason from our imagination—estranged it from our imagination by preventing it from making its own the unfettered single-minded pursuit of those great metaphysical themes whose myths and symbols have from time immemorial been the natural provender of all true art of the imagination and of all true knowledge.

What this means in purely practical terms is that we have to switch our reason from serving one set of premisses—one set of norms—to serving another; to switch it from serving the assumptions valid for the modern scientific mentality to serving the principles of sacred metaphysical doctrine. In so doing we will also automatically begin to reverse the process that has landed us in our present regions of desolation: we will begin once again to assess the validity or non-validity of statements made about the nature of the physical world—the created cosmos—not any longer according to the criteria effective for the modern scientific mentality but according to those inherent in sacred doctrine and sacred cosmologies.

We will begin once again to realize that when a poet like Dante speaks of the love that moves the sun and the other stars, or like Shakespeare of daffodils that take the winds of March with beauty, he is not speaking figuratively or in terms of hyperbole, or poetic licence, still less of pre-scientific ignorance; he is speaking of facts that are as literal and scientific as it is possible for a human being to speak of. We have to realize that everything about us is the work of intelligences and angels—enshrines the presence of intelligences and angels—and that there is a bond of kinship uniting our understanding and imagination to them so deep that it can be expressed only in terms of the deepest experience of our life. It is we who have violated that bond, dehumanizing ourselves in the process; but equally it is we who can and must reaffirm it. We can and must go to the fount of things, can and must make all things new. For however much we may appear to have debauched, abused and devastated the world that should have been our sacred trust, this world is still always what it is, still awaits to be reclaimed, transformed into its living image—a work that only the imagination can perform, and performs, when rightly conceived, with the assistance of art.

For the task of the artist—of the sacred artist—is to reveal to us and to itself the true nature of a world that we have allowed ourselves to regard as non-sacred, non-sacramental, merely neutral, if not simply dead or soulless matter; and to perform this task we do not have to retreat into some anterior or interior landscape of reverie or into the private world of dream. Neither do we have to project from our imagination various myths and symbols upon the outer, visible, demythologized world. Each thing contains within itself its own myth; it is in essence its own symbol, and is in itself a *dramatis persona* in that same cosmic play, that same mystery of birth, death and rebirth in which human life is also involved. Correctly seen, inner worlds are outer worlds, outer worlds are inner worlds. The sacred themes of art are immanent, and always have been immanent, in the *substantia rerum* of the world that offers itself to our perception. But to understand that we have not so much to raise the level of our consciousness, as to restitute it, restore it, set it right, by re-aligning it with the principles of a sacred cosmology, of a sacramental doctrine of creation, that will allow us to bring our imagination and our reason, the reality of myth and the reality of fact, once more into conjunction, into inner concord. For only by so doing can we heal the breach between art and metaphysics. Only thus can we recover the inner unity and harmony of our being.

And should it still be asked why such a re-alignment is so crucial that it may be said to constitute an indispensable condition of any genuine renewal of sacred art—indeed, of life itself—the answer is that since the course of art, as of life, follows always the course of thought—it is never the other way round—it must be that unless we first bring our thought into accord with the conceptual symbols of sacred realities we will not be able to bring our life, and hence still less our art, into accord with their imaginative symbols either. As Blake well knew, the first fight to be fought is the mental fight. And it was not for nothing that Blake also called the Holy Spirit—inspiration of all life as of all sacred art—an intellectual fountain.

Yet alignment with the principles of sacred doctrine,

however indispensable, is but the first step. Sacred doctrine is like purifying snow: it cleanses the mind of the obliquity and illusion with which it is otherwise filled and which prevent it from being able to possess even a theoretical knowledge of the Truth—and until it does possess that it cannot attain vision of the Truth itself. But to pass from such theoretical knowledge to actual spiritual vision requires a further step. It requires an inner transformation, a kind of dying to the concepts and intellectual symbols that constitute the world of our reason and a restitution—a regeneration—of our imagination itself.

For if it is our task to assist in that process whereby the imagination transmutes the spiritual into the corporeal, and the corporeal into the spiritual—celebrates the unending liturgy of epiphany and resurrection—then our imagination itself has to be able actually to perceive and experience the sacred dimension of all life. It has to open itself to the fructifying and transfiguring influx of the images of the spiritual world transmitted to it through the noetic or intellective power that alone in us is endowed with the capacity to apprehend their naked reality. Unless it does that our imagination cannot carry out its theophanic function, cannot reconcile the invisible and the visible, the spiritual and the physical, in a *unio mystica*, nor can its art initiate into vision, and so participate in that divine dramaturgy, that eternal cosmogony, in which God reveals Himself and knows Himself in all beings through being revealed in them and known by them.

Yet this noetic power—the spiritual intellect—itself cannot nourish our imagination with the images of the celestial archetypes unless it too is actualized—is activated. And this perhaps is the crux of all I have been saying. For although our imagination is our soul's organ of perception and experience, it cannot perceive or experience the sacred dimension of things unless it also becomes God's organ of perception. Paradox that it may sound, it is only the divine and what is divinized that can perceive and experience the divine. It is only in the divine light that the soul can see—see, that is to say, the inner reality of things, their inner love and beauty. It is only through the illumination of this light that the divine qualities of visible things are brought out, that each thing is invested with the theophanic function of its own divine archetype—actually becomes in some manner its own divine archetype—and reveals its angelic nature and presence.

For this light—'pure light, intellectual light', as Dante calls it[11]—is a spiritual energy, since only a spiritual energy can reveal in created things the beauty that manifests in visible form the divine beauty of the Creator. But beauty itself can be perceived in this hierophantic sense only through a divine love experienced as a love for the world so positive that it penetrates the whole natural order. And that which in the human being can experience such a love is the human heart. It is the heart therefore that is the seat, the organ, of the intellect—something that should convince us, if we need convincing, of how far the vision of the intellect is from being a matter of concepts and abstractions.

What, then, has to be actualized in the heart is the love that awakens in the intellect—the 'intellect of love',[12] the sword of prophecy—its latent power of vision. And what actualizes such love is prayer—the prayer of the spirit in which the activity of both our imagination and our reason is stilled. Such prayer is not a request for something. It is not an appeal. It is on the contrary a disposition of being that induces and permits the God who desires to reveal Himself to reveal Himself in our soul, divinizing our power of vision, and engendering in us the love and light that reconcile invisible and visible, metaphysical and physical, Creator and creation. It is only then that we perceive and experience the divine world in the human and natural world, the human and natural world in the divine world—in that world which is the source and the consummation of all sacred art and holy making, and which has itself no beginning and no end.

NOTES

1. *Convivio*, IV, 22.

2. *Inferno*, IX, 61–63

3. Letter 123 in *The Letters of John Keats*, ed. M. B. Forman (Oxford, 1935), p. 336.

4. W. B. Yeats, *Wheels and Butterflies* (London, 1934), p. 74, cited by Kathleen Raine in *Yeats the Initiate* (The Dolman Press, Mountrath, 1986), p. 106.

5. See in particular the works of Henry Corbin, *passim*.

6. See my *The Rape of Man and Nature* (Golgonooza Press, Ipswich, 1987) for a full account of this process.

7. By Aldous Huxley in 'The Substitutes for Religion', *Stories, Essays, Poems* (Everyman's Library), p. 284.

8. *Macbeth*, IV, i, 56–65.

9. For fuller discussion of this theme, see W. C. Curry's 'Tumbling Nature's Germens' in *Shakespeare's Philosophical Patterns* (Louisiana State University Press, 1959), pp. 29–49.

10. The degree to which the poetry of Hopkins and Eliot may be said to constitute sacred art is fully discussed by Harold L. Weatherby in his *The Keen Delight* (The University of Georgia Press, 1975), pp. 74–122. My brief assessment here is based entirely on Weatherby's conclusions.

11. *Paradisio*, XXX, 38.

12. Dante, *Vita Nuova*, XIX.

INDEX

✠

p 90 100

Lampert

Poetry